Servants on Horses

There is an evil I have seen under the sun,
an error which proceeds from the ruler.
Folly is set in high dignity, and the rich sit in low place.
I have seen servants on horses,
and princes walking as servants on the earth.

ECCLESIASTES 10 : 5-7

Yesterday this day's madness did prepare,
Tomorrow's triumph or despair.
— *The Rubai'yat of Omar Kha'yam*

Translations by Nina Cooper

Monsieur Lecoq by Emile Gaboriau
Published by Black Coat Press

Coming from Distinction Press

File No. 113 by Emile Gaboriau

The Omnibus Crime by Fortuné du Boisgobey

Servants on Horses

Nina Cooper

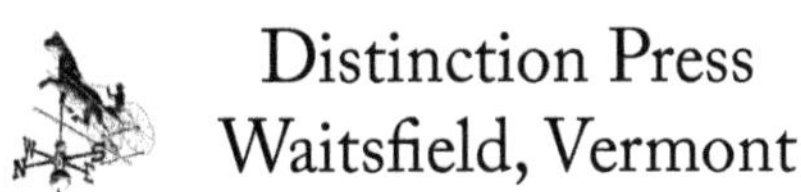

Distinction Press
Waitsfield, Vermont

Published by Distinction Press, LLC
PO Box 876, Waitsfield, Vermont 05673
802-496-3271 • www.distinctionpress.com

Cover design and layout by Kitty Werner, RSBPress, LLC

Cover photo by Kitty Werner of James Earle Fraser's sculpture *The End of the Trail* is used with permission, courtesy of the Shelburne Museum, Shelburne, Vermont. The original bronze sculpture can be seen at the Webb Gallery at the museum. www.shelburnemuseum.org

ISBN: 978-0-9802175-4-4

To

Jean Plummer Baker, Vlla tek (Golden Eagle),

descendant of both the

Muskogees (Choctaws) and Apaches

Contents

Acknowledgments

The encouragement and enthusiasm of my friend, Ethel Witsell, was instrumental in getting this novel published. I am most grateful for her efforts on my behalf.

Chapter I

Pitch Tree Settlement 1799–1811

Eva Bailey told this story. She said she would never have thought about telling it and would never have thought anyone would be interested in hearing or reading it until she was interviewed by the local county newspaper. The occasion of the interview was her upcoming birthday. She had outlived everyone in her family and in the earlier community. She was now a very, very old woman. The headlines of the article read:

SLIGHT EVA BAILEY CELEBRATES
93RD BIRTHDAY JUNE 6

CREDITS HARD WORK AND MODERATE
EATING FOR LONG LIFE

"The young reporter couldn't know," she reflected ironically, "that when I was born, June 6, 1866, the War of Secession had only recently ended, and by the time I was old enough to remember anything, my country was occupied by Federal troops come to 'Reconstruct' the South. Hard work and moderate eating were hardly options. So many adult men, and even boys as young as 13, had been killed in the war that women and children managed, if they were lucky, to barely survive by hard work in the fields. So little was produced during and immediately after the war that eating at all, much less 'moderate,' was considered a blessing.

Women whose husbands, fathers, and sons had not come back from the battlefields, or had come back so broken and weak they could not work, moved into the households of relatives, frequently as burdens.

Widows also frequently married men many years younger than themselves in order to keep their families and property together. Women marrying men ten, even twenty years younger than they, was not unusual. Her own father had survived the war, only to be killed by a Union officer in a dispute involving ownership of farmland.

Southern men who had participated in the Confederacy, in whatever way, were disenfranchised, so her father died from a Union officer's pistol shot and the farmland was given to her father's killer. She had grown up in the household of her grandfather with cousins, White, mixed-blood and full-blooded Muskogees. All their fathers had been killed fighting for the Confederacy. The males who lived were too young to protect and provide for families."

Since the newspaper reporter said those who did not know, the young or newcomers, would be interested, Eva worked with the young reporter and set down the story as her grandfather told it. He had kept letters of his own father and uncle, as well as newspaper articles both from New England and from his own Charleston and Savannah.

This is the story as her mixed-blood Muskogee/White grandfather told it to her and as the young newspaper reporter set it down. She said she told it neither with pride nor shame, or, rather, with both pride and shame, for her people, Muskogees and Whites, were on both sides of the conflict in the Indian Wars and in the War of Secession, some profiting and some losing.

"Set it down accurately," he had told Eva when she was of age but not yet married. "Never let our Muskogee people forget that the Devil, a man who embodied all the forces of pride, greed, duplicity, ignorance and hate, the Tennessee general and President of the United States, forced our people, the Creeks, now almost forgotten as a people, and sometimes called Cherokees, which they are not, to give up their homes and lands and to move to a foreign land west of the Mississippi. These lands had been ours for centuries, ever since we first migrated from the lands west of the Mississippi River and settled in what the Whites now call Georgia, Alabama, the Carolinas and Florida. When the Whites from Tennessee, Kentucky and the other states to the north of our people encroached more and more onto Creek and Cherokee lands, making and breaking treaties, stealing hunting grounds and fields, sometimes killing our men and raping our women, our people still tried to follow the White Man's laws.

"The Chiefs, the Miccos, petitioned the Federal government in Washington and the interpreter of the White Man's laws, the Justice John Marshall, to force the Federal government to stand by and honor the treaties made in good faith by the Muskogees, called The Five Civilized Tribes, and some of the best of the Whites. Justice Marshall found in our favor and told President Jackson that the treaties were valid and must be honored. He set down in writing to the President that no more White settlers could legally buy or sell or homestead on Muskogee lands. Jackson, in all his pride and greed defied the Justice and answered: 'He's made his decision. Now let him enforce it.' And so for the first time the separation of the powers of the Federal government as conceived by Thomas Jefferson and put into the Constitution of the United States of America failed."

And, as many of the very old, whose mind turns backward to what was, what might have been, and, based on the past, to what perhaps will be, the newspaper reporter continued Uriah's story as Eva told it to her.

Contrary to Justice Marshall's decision, Jackson lost no time and continued to move the Muskogees, the Cherokees, the Creeks and their smaller related tribes, west to Oklahoma, Mississippi, Arkansas, and Texas. Those who would not migrate died of starvation, assimilated with the White man, or fought guerrilla warfare against General Jackson and the Whites until most were either annihilated or finally sent by force west of the Mississippi River. The intermittent wars lasted more than forty years, from 1813 until 1858.

The Muskogees, Uriah said, had been invaded by the Spaniards, the French, and finally, the most enduring, as well as the ultimate cause of their destruction, by the Scots, the Irish, and the English, who came among them, not with an army, but one by one, living among them, marrying their women and, ultimately, at the end, choosing the way of the Whites and betraying the Muskogee.

Her people, the Creeks, could tell their descendants little of the time before the Scots and Irish. They could remember only that as a people they, and others with whom they later united, the Choctaws, Chickasaws, Cherokees, and Seminoles, had come from west of the Mississippi.

But her tribe, the Creeks, was the largest of what the Whites called The Five Civilized Tribes. They lived surrounded by the other Muskogee tribes, the Seminoles to the south, the Cherokees and Chickasaws to the north and northeast, and the Choctaws to the northwest.

As long as the oldest of the old men could remember, or their father's fathers could remember, they had lived in the tall pine forests, mountains and fresh streams of the country the Whites of the United States later called Alabama, Georgia, and the Carolinas. With their passion for organizing and classifying, the heads of these last invaders divided her people into Upper and Lower Creeks, depending on which side of a river they lived on. For many years both groups lived in peace with their brothers the Cherokees, the Choctaws, and the Chickasaws. The Seminoles, the last tribe to hold out against the White man and the only tribe never to surrender, were comprised of a mixture of many tribes as well as of runaway slaves.

But it is true that somewhat after the Colonies gained their independence from Great Britain, before her grandfather's time, the Cherokees had fought their brothers, the Creeks, in a battle for territory, pushing the Creeks south where they settled in her great-grandfather's time on both sides of the Chatahooche River. Those on the west side of the river were called Upper Creeks, centered and established around the Flint and Chattahoochee Rivers. Those on the east and central Georgia side were called Lower Creeks.

As a mixed breed Muskogee her grandfather had belonged to the Lower Creek Confederacy, first in North Georgia, and then to the Upper Creek Confederacy in central Alabama. He explained, "The division of the Creeks into separate groups was done by the Whites. All Creeks, all the Muskogees, belonged to the same nation and spoke the same language with only small differences between the tribes. In fact, the division of the Muskogees was not by geographic location, but by clan. Birth into a clan was determined by the mother. My people were composed of many clans, the Wind, the Bear, the Wildcat, and others. My mother was a member of the Wind Clan and I could join either the Wind Clan of the Upper or Lower Creeks without loss of status, since the clans crossed the boundaries of all the tribes. The clans had different rights and positions. The Wind Clan, the clan of my mother, had more rights and status than all the others. One of the important rights possessed by the Wind Clan concerned murder. All the clans except the Wind Clan had a limited time in which to punish murder, which was always punishable by death. The Wind Clan was not so limited and could punish murderers after many years. These rights and status were inherited and not earned, contrary to the way the rights and status of the Scotsmen who had come among them and represented their clans. The Scots had had to earn their rights and status by war or by strong personalities, but they recognized the clan organization when they came among the Muskogees. The Scotsmen called all the Muskogees 'forest folk,' 'coilltich,' and adjusted easily to the clan organization.

"The clans were represented in the same way in both the Upper and the Lower Creek territories as they were arbitrarily divided by the Whites. The clans from both sides were brothers through their clans. The Creeks were the largest of the Muskogees in the Five Civilized Nations and the ones who kept their customs and laws the longest and who resisted assimilation by the Whites longer than any others, except the Seminoles."

Eva, who took down this story from her grandfather, could not, however, claim to have no foreign blood, and many of those who did as the Whites took illegal possession of the Muskogee lands made the claim out of shame of their ancestry, or fear for their safety if they or their relations lived in the Territory. Any Indian blood, full, three-quarters, half, one-quarter, even one-eighth, even one-sixteenth, all made the person a Muskogee and as such he was deprived of rights the White man took for granted.

The blood of many Creeks, her grandfather told her, had long since been diluted. Each invader of Creek territory had taken what he wanted when he could, and what he wanted had always included women. But fortunately, the Creek Nation's customs were practical and able to include both those of pure Creek and those of foreign, mixed blood. Besides, after the Scots and Irish had been among them for some years, it was impossible to tell those of pure Creek and those of mixed blood. Even before the Scots and Irish, other foreign blood had been mixed with that of the Muskogees, since the Spanish and the French had preceded the Whites from Britain or the Colonies.

"In former times," Uriah said, "the Muskogee Creeks had no surnames. Before the Scots, the Irish, and the English came, every child belonged to his mother's family and clan. Her brothers were responsible for their sister and were also responsible for the upbringing and training of their sister's children. The father, after he had planted his seed, had few rights over the woman. One of the few was punishment for adultery. He had neither rights over nor responsibility for the offspring of the union. The man could take other wives if he chose, but he had to ask his wife's permission. Failure to do so was considered adultery and was punishable by the first wife's brothers or male clan members. Men, however, were forbidden to marry within their own clan. For many years both the Creeks and the White man found this arrangement satisfactory. It avoided many of the unnecessary worries of the White man. No stigma was attached to the woman however the copulation and resulting conception occurred, either by rape or by mutual consent. The Scots and the Irish, and sometimes the English, changed this old, old custom of the Creeks."

Long after Uriah's death, Eva was to remember his words. When the Muskogees, those of the Seminoles in Florida had almost perished, in the White men's twentieth century, men of Washington insisted that the women these foreigners took could give only a Muskogee first name and that the family name of the Scotsman, the Irishman, or the Englishman, or the American who fathered the child had to be attached as the family name. This situation was not to the advantage of the Muskogee child, because the clan, or family, of his father, Scots, Irish, British or from the former Colonies, was far away, and sometimes forgotten by the men who retained their ancient clan name but little else. The mother's brothers, either in resentment or in parsimony, sometimes claimed that the child who bore the foreigner's name was the responsibility of the White man, who also frequently claimed no responsibility for him. The McDonalds, the MacInnis, the McGillivrays, the McIntoshs, the McDavids, the Pearsons, the Powells, the Hawkins, the Moniacs, the Tates, and others took Creek women and, after a generation or two, the Creek name was dropped and the Irish, the Scots or the English added a foreign first name to the Scots or Irish or English surname and the Creek language and customs began to disappear.

However, Eva remembered her grandfather's words with pride when, long after the Creeks had been displaced and sent into exile west of the Mississippi, more than a hundred years after the birth of her grandfather, and here she called him by both his English and his Muskogee name, Uriah/Sakoeka, the remnant of his people in Florida refused to obey the White man's rules. Some of the brothers of the Creeks, the Seminoles, particularly the women, kept the old ways and refused to accept the law of the White man which would force them to take the surname of their husbands or the father of their child, abandoning the custom of the Muskogee, and, if there was no husband who would give a surname, to register their children as bastards. The White man's Department of the Interior, Commission to the Five Civilized Tribes, Muskogee, Indian Territory, when they tried to take a census of the Seminoles, sent a record to Washington in 1902:

> *It is a well-known fact that many Indian women continue after marriage to use their maiden names and some of these appearing before the Commission have refused to permit their*

enrollment under the surnames of their husbands. In other instances, objection was made to giving an illegitimate child the name of his father and in numerous cases it was insisted upon by applicants and tribal officers that parties had no surname and would never be identified by a surname and so they were arbitrarily enrolled with the given name by which they had always been known.

And so the Seminole Census of 1902 carries Seminoles of full blood and those of mixed blood, both those with Muskogee names and those with White names.

Her Muskogee/Irish grandfather was the first of his clan to drop his Muskogee/Seminole name, Sakoeka, a Seminole name given by his Creek mother in honor of a Seminole friend, and to become Uriah, a name which did not identify him as a Muskogee Creek.

Much, much later, when he was a very old man, after the War of Secession, he would ironically recall, when telling his granddaughter about the old days, about what happened in that long ago past, "Missy, I'm probably one of the few men still alive who lost his land twice to the White man. I lost it once when I was a Muskogee of the Wind Clan of the Creeks, and once when I was a White man of the Confederacy. The first time I lost it to Governor Troup of Georgia and General Andrew Jackson of Tennessee and that half-breed William McIntosh, and the second time to the Carpetbaggers of the North and the Federal Army of Occupation which came to 'Reconstruct' the South. Few men here could be on the losing side twice in one lifetime, but remember, Missy, I said, 'losing side,' not 'wrong side.'"

Her Irish great grandfather, Daniel Pearson, father of Uriah/Sapoeka, came first, at 17, to the Carolinas with his brother, John, 16, and then to Georgia, where at 21, he married, with her brothers' blessings, a 13-year-old Creek of the Wind Clan. At the birth of his first Creek/Irish son, he sought the advice of an old Irish itinerant priest, who was passing through the Pitch Tree settlement, now Atlanta, Georgia, as to a name. He inclined towards the names Johoiakim and Uriah, but couldn't decide between the two. The itinerant priest, Father O'Connor, tried to dissuade him from either, "Neither is a good choice, my son. Remember, Johoiakim was a wicked King of Israel who killed one Uriah for criticizing him and bringing bad news and another Uriah lost his wife to David, the great King of Israel, who also saw to it that Uriah, the Hittite, was put in the thick of the fight and killed in battle.

Irish in its skepticism, her great-grandfather's replied, "There can't be much in a name. I'm named Daniel Pearson, and I don't expect to be thrown into a pit with lions. Besides, my father was named David and he couldn't hoe enough potatoes in Erin to keep the twelve members of our family fed. King and mighty man he certainly was not. As for the name Johoiakim, if fathers feared to name their sons after wicked kings, they would never choose George, Charles, William, or many another name of a king or mighty man who was no better than he should have been and who took no thought of his people that God had given him to rule over and protect."

To that the priest could make no reply. They decided that Uriah was easier to spell and pronounce than Johoiakim, so the child was baptized Uriah, carrying with him the destiny of all those mixed blood Pearson/Creek generations following.

In the spring and summer following the birth of Uriah, Daniel Pearson had planted and harvested a crop of corn, sweet potatoes, peas and squash on the communal land allotted him by his wife's clan, a condition required by the clan to consider the marriage valid. Prior to the birth of his son Daniel Pearson lived, as was the Muskogee custom, in one of the houses of his mother-in-law. Each family had four houses.

a winter house, a summer house, a warehouse and a granary. After his son's birth, his brothers-in-law helped him build his own dwelling near his wife's people, adjacent to the central communal square.

The house was rectangular, practical and permanent. The floor was hard ground; the sides which supported the top were made of six-feet high oak limbs. Smaller limbs and branches of more limber and supple trees such as the willow were woven through the oak posts, which were then dabbed and caulked with red clay mixed with pine straw, which hardened into a solid wall. Straw mixed with the red clay made a weather-tight building. When the red clay was smeared and smoothed down the sides of the building, it produced a colorful red, beige and dark brown house. The top was of hand-hewn cedar shakes covered with palmetto branches which created a slanted, peaked roof. Cooking and washing were done in a separate house, built in a similar fashion, and used by the entire clan. In the winter the old and the very young also used the cooking and washing houses as sleeping quarters because they were warmer than the individual houses. Council meetings were held in another house on the central communal square. Daniel Pearson built his trading post just outside the village on the Federal road at the conjunction of the Federal road and the Creek hunting and trading paths.

Sapehunka, Muskogee wife of Daniel Pearson, retained her given name, never agreeing to take her husband's surname, a foreign one, nor would she convert to the religion of her husband, although she did not forbid Daniel Pearson's having their son baptized in the religion of his Irish forefathers. Nevertheless, resisting calling her son Uriah, she gave him instead the Seminole name Sakoeka, in honor of a friend among the Seminoles as she herself was named for her mother's Seminole friend, a name which identified Uriah from his birth in 1799 until he quit his birthplace in 1811.

Daniel Pearson, when he first arrived with his brother in the Carolinas, had trapped for a living. For several years the two managed both to earn not only enough for subsistence, but for a fair living and to save a little money, as well as to send a little back to their family in Ireland. But, four or five years after they arrived, the Carolinas became too crowded with trappers, game became scarce, and theft and fights over territory become more and more troublesome. Daniel left the Carolinas after four years for North Georgia, but John remained for several more years in North Carolina and later transferred his growing trading business to South Carolina. In Georgia, Daniel, realizing that he knew much less than the Muskogees in the Pitch Tree Lower Creek area where they had settled and lived for thousands of years, found it more profitable to trade with the Creeks for pelts instead of trapping in a country not his own, running the risk of intruding on Creek lands and into difficulties with Muscogee trappers. Married to a Muskogee of the Wind Clan, he was accepted among them and life continued much as it had been in North Carolina. Uriah/ Sakoeka and his mother as Muskogee members of the Wind Clan guaranteed protection to Daniel also.

However, as Uriah/Sakoeka's neared his twelfth birthday, in 1811, there were rumors of a new invasion of the Colonies by Great Britian. Daniel Pearson, who, in the intervening years had become one of the major fur traders of the region, trusted by the Muskogee and the White man alike, successfully steered a path between the Upper and Lower Creeks as well as the Irish, Scots, and Whites from the former Colonies. In late 1811, however, the rumors seemed to be becoming fact. News from abroad, although sometimes several months late in arriving to the South, seemed to confirm Britain's intention to regain her North American colonies. Many of the Muskogees saw this possibility as offering protection by the British against the White men from Kentucky, Tennessee, the Carolinas, and Georgia encroaching daily on Muskogee lands A general Council meeting of both Upper and Lower Muskogees was held in the Pitch Tree area. (The area around present-day Atlanta had no peach trees. The street so-named there was a corruption of pitch tree, named for the resin of the pine tree.) There was much debate about what position the Creeks should take should the British invade.

The custom of the Muskogee was to send sticks painted red to villages to indicate a decision for war. Those in agreement were Red Stick Warriors. At the general Council meeting, the Pitch Tree Muskogees were being swayed by Red Stick Warriors, some favoring joining the British, some advising joining the Americans. Those favoring joining the Americans were followers of the half breed Muskogee/British William McIntosh, Chief of the Coweta Village Muskogees of the Lower Creeks. Communication between the Muskogee Creeks in Alabama and the Red Stick Warriors in Coweta Village of Georgia continued weekly. Mixed-breed warriors were more eager and ready for war with the White man than were many full-blooded Muskogees. Daniel Pearson, in his deliberations with the elder of his two brothers-in-law, had stressed the value of neutrality. Following Muskogee custom, his elder brother in-law had been given a second name after his personality had been perceived as being consistent. He traded his birth name, given by his mother, for the name Hoponika Futsakia, Truth Teller.

Since Creek custom did not allow White men to attend council deliberations, Daniel urged Hoponika Futsakia, a member of the Council, as were all males of the clan, to try to persuade his brothers of the benefits of neutrality.

"You know the White men here from the Carolinas, Kentucky, Tennessee and those who have settled here from across the wide water. Some of them you can, and do, trust. However, their battles are not your battles. You live in peace with those who are honest. You know those who cheat and steal. What do you know of the British? They rule the land of my fathers and have for many years taken anything of value there. My people, the Irish, have learned their language and obeyed their laws, and yet we aren't equal to them in any way. You say you are surrounded by the White men here who grow more numerous and greedy year after year. That's true, but will the British be different? They are the same people as the men here, only removed a few generations, just as you are of the same blood as your brothers the Seminoles. The Seminoles dwell with the Spanish to the south of your land. Neither the Spanish nor the British will aid you. And the people of the colonies promise to do so, but may not or, perhaps, cannot help you once they have gained what they seek.

"The Great White Father in Washington has trouble with the separate states because some states say they are free to govern their territory and to deal with the Muskogee as they like. Their Constitution has existed only a few years. They ignore the words of the far-away government in Washington. The Spanish in the lands south of you are growing weak and giving their claim to the stolen Muskogee lands there to the United States. When they have ceded the rest, you'll be bound on the north and the south by the White man. Do not join either side. Wait for one or the other side to ask for your help. Then, when they realize they need your help, you may negotiate and have a better chance peacefully to stop losing hunting grounds and villages. Besides, the Creeks are the largest of the Five Civilized Tribes. It would be to the advantage both of the former colonies and of the British to divide you from your brothers the Cherokees and Choctaws and from your even nearer brothers, dividing the Upper and Lower Creeks, creating civil war among you. If they divide you, your advantage in numbers will count for nothing. And therefore they will try to divide you."

Truth Teller carried Daniel Pearson's words to the Council, giving him credit for the beliefs expressed but adding that he thought his brother-in-law's words were true. This reasoning was opposed by the Red Stick Warriors of both the Upper and the Lower Creeks. They saw some truth in what he said, but even greater truth in the reply to the Whites by the great Tucumseh, a Shawnee, whose mother was Creek. Tucumseh had traveled from his home on the Ohio River through all the tribes down to the Muskogees trying to unite them against the encroachments of the White man. His message was the question:

"Where today are the Pequot, the Narrangaset and the Mohicans and many other once powerful tribes of our people? They have vanished before the avarice and oppression of the White man as snow before a summer sun."

The Red Stick warrior who reminded the Council of Tecumseh's words, an Upper Creek Talladega Muskogee, replied to Truth Teller, "He's a White man and he reasons like a White man. His origins are far away. If his people had fought better and longer, they might have been able to keep their language and their lands. He might now be in his own land and not in the land of the Muskogees. This land belongs to the Muskogees here, as the lands to the south of us belong to the Seminoles, our brothers. The oldest of the old men cannot remember when we did not fish and hunt and trap here. Our oldest stories tell of our life here from almost the beginning of time. Why should we negotiate with the White man to keep what is ours? Even if we were forced to negotiate, could we trust him? The word of the Great White Father in Washington is, with each new treaty, violated by the White men here who call our land Alabama or Georgia, who say that the government in Washington does not in all things govern them. They say they are free to make treaties and laws governing the Muskogee, the Cherokees, the Choctaws, the Chickasaws and the Seminoles in many things and to buy and take the land of the Muskogee as they like whenever they want or need it. They say they are free to deal with the Muskogee as they choose and do not have to honor the treaties made in Washington. They say the States keep some of their sovereign rights and give only part of their rights to the Great White Father and the government in Washington. If the Great White Father will not, or cannot, protect our land and rights, then we must fight."

When it was clear that the Red Stick Warriors would win the debate, although it was not clear if the Upper Creeks would join the Americans as the Lower Creek Coweta Creeks urged, Daniel Pearson decided to send his son to South Caroline to his brother. Sapehunka had produced two additional children, both girls, who were too young to go to South Carolina. Daniel told Sapehunka, who, by Muskogee law, would have to agree, that he wanted to send Uriah/Sakoeka to a South Carolina school to learn the skills of the White man, reading and writing, and the knowledge of numbers. Sapehunka protested that these skills were useless in a Muskogee village. Nothing good could come of them, only the desire to follow the greedy, bad paths of the White men.

To this Daniel replied, "What I've seen and can judge of Uriah's leanings, I think he will return to the Muskogees. He prefers hunting, fishing, trapping, and wrestling with the other boys to the few simple lessons that I've been able to give him. He will probably learn so ill that you'll never recognize much book learning in him at all. In any case, he's now too much persuaded by the Red Sticks. Young as he is, he may, when trouble and war come, be old enough to join the Red Sticks. It's clear that some of those in the Lower Creek Coweta Village will join the Tennesseans. William McIntosh, Micco of the Coweta Creeks, although half-British, is already allied with the Tennesseans."

Even as he was trying to persuade his wife and her brothers to send Uriah/Sapoeka to a White school, Daniel Pearson tried one last time to persuade his wife's village by way of her brother, Truth Teller, to avoid taking sides in the impending war between the British and their former colonies. He admitted the truth of the situation which the Red Stick warriors had stressed. "You're right to say the White men are already dividing the land into individual pieces, contrary to the custom of the Muskogees, who share all the land. But, if the Upper Creeks, your brothers and friends, fight, they will join the British, who will lose. The news we get from across the wide waters tells that the British do not agree they have lost the last war with the Whites here of the former colonies. But, nevertheless, they have other battles in Europe, right now more important, which take their time and money. They will not be able to give enough time or money to fight the former colonies. When they and their Allies have won the war with the Frenchman, Napoleon, they will turn again to invading this continent. Whether the Upper or Lower Creeks fight either with the White men of the United States or with the British, all Muskogees will lose sooner or later."

Moderate Muskogees, seeing the truth on both sides, met in Council, and in an effort to keep their lands without going to war either with the British or the former Colonies, passed a law forbidding any Muskogee from selling any more land to the White man on either side of the Chatahooche River. Sapehunka and her brother, Truth Teller, had remained neutral, joining neither the Upper nor the Lower Creek Red Stick Warriors. Sapehunka's younger brother, however, barely older than Sakoeka/Uriah, joined the Upper Creek Red Stick warriors who would soon fight in Alabama.

When Daniel Pearson decided to send his son away from the forthcoming hostilities, Uriah was almost 13 years old. Much later, however, when the White man began to take a census including mixed breeds, he alternately gave his birth date as 1798 or 1799, saying that neither his father or mother could remember his exact birth date. At first, he refused to leave the land of the Muskogee and his decision was supported both by his mother and her brothers. By Muskogee law Daniel Pearson had no paternal rights over his son. He reasoned with them, at first patiently and then with greater and greater anger and frustration.

To Uriah/Sakoeka he said, "The world of the Muskogee is changing quickly. You must be able to change with it. Young as you are, you already have the skills necessary to live as a Muskogee Creek. Your uncles have taught you well. You are almost as skillful with a knife and bow as they are. As for the use of firearms, you learned that early. But, though you can and do speak English with me, it's faulty and no one would think you English. You can translate for the Muskogees who come into the trading posts and help them to be sure they're not being cheated. This is to speak English but ill and you can do nothing more complex in English. If you go into the White man's world for a short while, you can be equal to him in the skills which both he and you need to be accepted, to gain favor, and to succeed as a White man. Once you command those skills you can return to the land of the Muskogee and live like a Muskogee if you choose. You'll be of greater use to your mother's people with the White man's knowledge and skills."

Sapoeka, his mother, and his uncles were finally persuaded and reluctantly prepared for his journey to the Carolinas. To prepare Sakoeka, who had lived almost thirteen years as a Muskogee, for the world of the White man was not easy. Each time it seemed he might be prepared there arose another stumbling block. First, there was the question of the White man's clothes. Like his uncles, Sakoeka wore in summer a breech cloth and in winter long trousers, both made from soft doe skin cured by the women of the clan. In cold weather he wore, carelessly, cotton shirts made by the women of the clan from cloth bought at the trading posts, or European made shirts, if trapping had been good and there was much money from pelts or deer skins. Occasionally he wrapped a brightly colored piece of material around his head as a turban and, sometimes, adorned himself with a feather in the turban. Much of the year he did not wear shoes. When he did, they too were made of deer skin cured by the clan's women. In preparation for his journey into the White man's world, Daniel Pearson had sent away for a suit of clothes and black leather button-up shoes in the latest fashion. These, Sakoeka refused to wear. He said the suit of clothes was hot and restraining and the shoes hurt his feet. Although he put the suit of clothes on several times he did not promise to wear it. Up until the day of his departure he refused to wear the White man's shoes.

Daniel Pearson thought it wise to warn him about the White man's dress and some of his customs. Although he had seen Irish and Scots traders and trappers for most of his life, these dressed almost the same way as the Muskogee. Indeed, many were of mixed blood and still lived in their mother's village. Daniel Pearson told his son, "The White man wears not only a suit of clothes and shoes, but he also sometimes carries a stick which he calls a cane, even though he may not be crippled or need a stick to lean on. He may also carry a watch on a chain which he puts in a little pocket in his trousers. He usually wears a black or brown hat which he takes off when he meets someone he wants to honor, or meets women. His women do not, as do the women of your mother's clan, and any Muskogee woman, show the tops of their bodies without clothes. White women are not as practical as your mother and her cousins and sisters, who, if it is hot, wear only the lower part of their bodies covered. The top part of the White man's woman cannot be touched by a stranger and it is always covered. There also certain natural things which the Muskogee talk about freely but which the White man finds shameful. You must not talk about relieving yourself and you must never relieve yourself where others can see you. If you watch carefully, you'll learn without being told the other peculiarities of the White man."

Two months or so before Sakoeka's departure, Daniel Pearson wrote to his brother:

Dear Brother,

First, let me tell you how grateful I am that you have agreed to find a school for Uriah. As I told you, I'd like to give him as good an education as our poor father, with much trouble and expense that he could ill afford, gave you and me. The poor babes who followed us, eight of them, were not so fortunate. Although our education was simple, it was strong. In the school of the Brothers he chose, we were taught much above our station. Our knowledge of Latin and Greek is better than that of some gentlemen. When we wish, we can pass for educated men.

Uriah will not be an easy pupil. It's not that he can't learn readily. Indeed, he learns almost everything rapidly. The problem is that he has been brought up by his mother, who adores and spoils him, and his uncles in their Muskogee Wind Clan. He is a very good Muskogee. He rides, he shoots with a bow and arrow accurately, wields a knife expertly, knows the use of firearms and can hunt and trap as well as any of them. He sometimes helps at the trading posts, but there he is not expert. As a Muskogee, he distrusts the White man and sometimes insults him. When I tax him with his behavior, he always pretends that the insult was made in ignorance. Sometimes it was, but frequently it is done deliberately. Whatever school you may find for him will have to deal with this attitude. This is, in fact, one of the reasons I want him to go into the White man's world. If events continue as they are, he'll not have the luxury of living as a Muskogee, and therefore must learn not to insult the White man, or, at least, become more expert and veiled in his insults.

Please let me know if you can help me in this matter. If you look for a school, I prefer a school that gives some religions instruction. His mother has seen to his instruction in the religion of the Muskogee, a religion which will not harm him and cannot interfere with any other religion.

Your Brother,
Daniel Pearson

A month after his letter, Daniel Pearson received a reply.

Dear Brother,

Yes, my mind holds and I'll help find a school for Uriah. However, my situation has changed a little. As you know, I've been trading mainly with the Cherokees, but also somewhat with the Creeks for pelts and deer skins. I have, in turn, sold these in Charleston, and with the liquid money I have bought cloth and other goods there from Ireland and England. The trade in cloth is now centered in Charleston and Savannah. I have made regular trips to Charleston for the purpose of establishing a few reputable contacts to serve as intermediaries for me to sell the pelts and skins at a higher price than I can get here in the Territory. I intend in the following weeks to go to Charleston and spend as much time there as is necessary to find a reliable contact. What I suggest to you is that you let me find a good family in Charleston with whom Uriah can lodge for several months until I finish my business there and during that time he attend school in Charleston or in its vicinity.

The city is growing rapidly and offers much in the way of education, not only in established schools, but in knowledge of commerce and society. In anticipation that you'll agree with my suggestions, I've examined the religious establishments in Charleston. I feel you would prefer a Catholic school, but the Catholics have only recently come into this part of South Carolina, perhaps as recently as ten or twenty years ago and, very poor, they do not as yet have any schools except at the elementary level. The major religious establishments seem to be Hebrew, Presbyterian, and Methodist. The Hebrews have excellent academic training for the young, but probably both they and you would find a third religious philosophy too confusing to a Muskogee. The Presbyterians are numerous and have good academies, in fact, probably the best at this time. However, the discipline is stern and allows for flogging for mistakes or misjudgments. I should like your opinion on that, for you tell me Sakoeka is likely, according to the White man's rules, to need correction from time to time. The Methodists, on the other hand, have been here a long time. Their leader, John Wesley, a Swiss Frenchman, preached here about a century ago. They have a large church in Savannah, and they have spread throughout the Carolinas, and they are, therefore, firmly established in the society of Charleston, although their schools are possibly somewhat inferior in the classical languages to those of the Presbyterians.

Please let me know your thoughts. We'll make firm plans when I know your preferences. I send my best regards to you, your wife and children.

Your brother,
John Pearson

The gist of his brother's letter Daniel talked over with his wife and her brothers. The brothers were against any religious instruction. The religious White men they had met they thought hypocritical and often cruel without reason. They had found that the White men often excused their unnecessary cruelty in the name of their religion. Their sister, however, was less apprehensive. Sapehunka and her sisters had taught the Muskogee religious philosophy to Sakoeka and she felt that he would not accept a contrary religion easily. To the Muskogee, all life was sacred and he did not attack or kill unless, like the wild animal, he needed food or needed to protect himself or his own. His family was to be honored and protected; his friends helped if they were in need and he was not to lie or steal. This was a summary of what he had been taught.

At the end of many discussions, it was decided that Uriah should be educated by the Presbyterians. Although Daniel Pearson preferred the best education that could be had, he had severe reservations as to flogging. It was not that Sakoeka/Uriah would not, according to the White man's standards, need that punishment... He told his brother, John, that Sakoeka was stubborn and would accept instruction only if it was reasonable and he could see the purpose and use of it. As for flogging, as a Muskogee, especially a Muskogee of the Wind Clan, he would never accept that another should treat him as a slave. No Muskogee had ever been a slave. An American general who should know, himself part Creek, had written, much later when Sakoeka/Uriah was a grown man,

> *Not one Indian, male or female, in 100, but would put an end to their existence, rather than submit to such treatment. Even as late as 1836, I knew several Indian women who, rather than risk their children under the control of the Emigrating Indian Agent, put them to death, some of them large enough to walk, and these women had long been acquainted with the Whites. In fact, I knew two men kill themselves in Montgomery, rather than move, when their whole townspeople were along and not in any danger whatever.*

Even the black slaves of the Muskogee, of which there were many, were not flogged often, and only for the gravest of crimes. Besides, he wrote, he feared that if someone attempted to flog Sakoeka, his son would try to kill that person, and might possibly succeed. Therefore, it would probably be wise to discuss the situation with whoever was head of the Presbyterian school chosen to see if they thought Sakoeka could be controlled or if they would accept that he be expelled instead of flogged, if, in their judgment, the need arose, or if they would be willing to try. If they refused him entry, the next choice would be the Methodists. Failing that, perhaps some tutor could be found to give instruction in languages and mathematics at a higher level than he had at present.

He heard again from his brother in a few weeks saying that it would not be necessary that Sakoeka go so far as Charleston to enter a good school because he had heard of an excellent school in a village outside and north of the city, closer to his Georgia home. The Headmaster was reputed to be a very manly man, stern, fair, respected by his students, and academically sound. Living accommodations were provided for the students. However, there was a problem in that the person recommending the school said that students were trained to do chores, both domestic and in the field, helping with farming, and hunting to provide food for the entire school. He understood that Sakoeka's uncles and mother, as well as the rest of her family and her clan, owned black slaves who did much of the manual labor, as well as the cooking and cleaning. Sakoeka would not be exempt from such work because the headmaster believed that such training was good both for the body and for the soul. He asked Daniel's opinion as to whether he should proceed with negotiations for trying to enroll Sakoeka in that school.

Again, Daniel sought the consent of his wife and his brothers-in-laws. They differed, the younger of the two uncles violently opposing that Sakoeka should be subjected to such an indignity as flogging and required to do domestic labor, or to enter a school which condoned such things, the other siding with the mother, who said that since they had already agreed that he might profit from the White man's learning, they would try to persuade Sakoeka to try the White man's strange ways. However, they all agreed in steadfastly opposing that he should be flogged, preferring expulsion instead.

Daniel wrote again to his brother explaining his wife's and her brothers' decision. In reply, his brother said that he had visited the school and he gave further details. The head of the school, he said, was a Presbyterian minister, educated in a South Carolina academy, although his father was Irish, as were he and Daniel. The school gave a classical education, concentrating on Greek, Latin, mathematics, and English. There were also daily lessons in theology. Each student was required to take all of these courses. In addition, lessons in surveying were given to those who wished it. The students were required to help with domestic chores, such as cleaning their quarters, but might pay a slave to wash their clothes. Help with the kitchen garden was also required, as was helping to provide meat for the entire school and for the table of the head of the school, since the Head Master did not have sufficient time after teaching to hunt and trap. Food was simple but ample. The wife of the headmaster and her kitchen help prepared corn bread and vegetables daily, but meat was served only three or four days a week and consisted of bacon from the school's hogs and game supplied by the students taking turns hunting and trapping. The living accommodations for students were in three large dormitories which housed up to 40 or 50 students, who slept on plain beds constructed against the wall. The mattresses for the beds came from the cotton grown on the farm. These accommodations, he said, were probably as good or superior to those of his mother and her family. The head of the school, his wife, and their two small sons lived in a large log cabin with a detached kitchen and there were also out buildings for livestock. Lessons were held outdoors and students prepared their lessons there also in good weather. Two large log cabins served as meeting places and as lecture and homework rooms in bad weather.

The head of the school himself was a tall, rather plain man, with a serious, but not forbidding manner. He dressed as a gentleman of good family, but not ostentatiously. His wife was a pretty woman with genteel manners. It was said that she was related to plantation families in Virginia. Both gave the air of being responsible, trustworthy and kind. In general, he was impressed both with the school and its director. He suggested that Uriah meet him in Charleston and remain with him until he had completed his business there. This would give Uriah an opportunity to see a large, busy city as well as the seaport. After he had finished his business he would accompany Uriah to the school, introduce him to the head of the school and arrange for his matriculation. All of this was agreed upon and Uriah prepared to leave to become a White.

While the second war between the former Colonies and Britain, and the civil war among the Upper and Lower Creeks was brewing, but not yet begun, Sakoeka would meet his uncle, John Pearson, in Charleston on the wharves and go with him to the school. Although private ownership of property had not yet become common among the Muskogee, some among the Lower Creeks had begun to settle permanently on pieces of tribal land, fencing it and planting large sections, and harvesting these sections without sharing with the rest of the clan in violation of the custom of the Muskogee. As Sakoeka and the trappers went through north Georgia into South Carolina, he saw this greedy, selfish, custom of the White man adopted by some of the Muskogees and did not approve. The further they progressed towards Charleston the more the country changed. At first the Muskogee he saw kept the pole, stick and mud houses of his ancestors which provided separate dwellings for sleeping, for cooking, for washing and for clan meetings.

The activities in these Creek villages continued much the same as in his own village at the Pitch Tree settlement. There, as Sakoeka had prepared to leave and left with the trappers, some of the women were busy sweeping the area surrounding the houses with brush brooms, which the Whites who kept the custom called "brish brooms." Others were working in small kitchen gardens behind the houses. Still others were cooking meals or grinding smoked tobacco leaves into a fine powder into which they then dabbed small brushes made from green hackberry tree twigs, the ends of which had been chewed until they became very soft. Some of these they gave to the old men who sat outside the houses or on the communal square. The old men used the soft ends of the twig brushes either to clean their teeth or to put some of the ground tobacco under their tongues. Some of the women themselves placed the twigs' ends dipped in ground tobacco into their mouths, usually under the tongue. Both the women and the men who dipped the ground tobacco had tobacco stains around the mouth and sometimes down the chin. The White man had taken up the habit and called the powdered tobacco leaves "snuff."

Family activities and grooming took place in front of the sleeping houses or on the communal square. Women combed and braided their own and children's hair. Girls gathered pine straw and wove it into small baskets for carrying eggs, berries and fruit. Old men, men too old for trapping or hunting, split thin pieces of oak into strips to be woven into larger baskets to carry vegetables, game, fish, or cotton. Men and adolescent boys walked from the village down well-worn paths which led to fields or hunting grounds. Boys too young for trapping or hunting played kick ball or stick ball or chase in the village square. This life Sakoeka left with regret.

Somewhat further, the communal houses were sparse and the villages almost empty, although the houses were built the same as those in Sakoeka's village. These were new villages, since the custom of the Muskogee was to start a new village when any village had begun to have 300 to 400 hundred inhabitants Somewhat later, however, the building method changed, combining Muskogee buildings with the White man's buildings. The houses became one or two room log cabins. Some were inhabited by Muskogees, but most were mixed breed Muskogees or White families. Muskogees still slept and cooked separately, building smaller log, stick, and mud houses for cattle and feed stuffs. But here the houses, outbuildings, pastures and fields were frequently fenced with split-rail fences. Still, the fields were the same crops, sweet potatoes, peas, corn, squash. Even further on, the Muskogee mud, stick and pole houses and outbuildings disappeared entirely, as did most of the Muskogees, both the mixed breed and the full blooded Muskogee. Nearing the Ashley River, on the outskirts of Charleston, there were only log cabins, some still with one or two rooms, but others incorporating the kitchen into the main cabin and adding a separate bedroom or a lean-to. Very near Charleston the houses became much bigger, more imposing, and were made of planed, painted wood, or even brick and stone. Sakoeka/Uriah saw these changes with wonder and disapproval.

The journey across Georgia and into South Carolina took them at first through forests, inhabited only by an occasional group of deer and a lone Creek or Cherokee. When they entered or approached small settlements the scene began to change. There were few women doing cleaning chores. The areas around houses were not cleaned and brushed free of debris. The buildings, rough log cabins notched by hand and not intended as dwellings, crowded each other along a narrow path and in general had few Creeks. Instead of women doing manual labor and household chores, men were busy pursuing activities first learned years before from the English or from European nations. Some were working in smithies, laboring to repair old or create new wheels, bells, fittings for harnesses, guns, and, occasionally gates and fences. Others were working at lasts where new shoes were being made to order, or repairing worn leather soles. Gunsmiths worked near the smiths and occasionally the smith and the gunsmith were one and the same. There were more full-blooded

Whites and few Muskogees of either mixed or full blood. The buildings were for use in a trade and for storage of goods. Men shouted back and forth to each other, dogs barked, horses and carts passed each other with occasional wrangling among the occupants as to right of way on the roughly defined road. Rough log cabins advertised lodgings while others advertised whiskey. The few women to be seen were delivering food to the workmen or buying goods offered for sale in make-shift stalls beside the road.. There were more dogs than children. A few black slaves worked with the White men, the slaves doing most of the manual labor.

The nearer they came to Charleston, the closer and closer to each other were settlements of this kind. Everyone who saw Sakoeka, who had not changed into his White man's clothes, looked at him with suspicion and disdain. He, in turn, returned their glances with the same haughtiness he would have given a slave. His entry into the White man's world would not have a peaceful beginning.

Chapter II

Charleston, South Carolina
Summer 1811

The group Daniel Pearson put together to take Sakoeka to Charleston began with two traders with whom Daniel had often done business and whom he trusted. One was Sapehunka's brother, his elder uncle, a full-blooded Creek. He, like some Muskogees, had several names in his lifetime. The first was given by his mother or her brothers at his birth. One name, or more, later, he would earn as his personality developed or as he merited a different name either by his actions or his inactions. Sakoeka's older uncle, when he became an adult, was named Hoponika Futsakia, Truth Teller in English. Throughout his life he lived up to his second name.

The other was a mixed blooded Creek of Negro and Creek ancestry named Mabry. His father, a freed slave, had chosen to live among the Muskogee because, he said, he was tired of the lies of the White man and the Muskogees didn't lie. Mabry had grown up in the Pitch Tree village with the Creeks and considered himself a member of the clan of his mother, a Creek.

These men had been entrusted not only with Daniel's son Uriah, but also with pelts and deer skins to be sold for one of several types of currency in use, the United States not yet having an established uniform national currency in general use. They might also be bartered for cloth and domestic articles later to be sold or bartered at the trading post for more skins or pelts, making a profit at each transaction. The three completed about half the journey alone. However, as the party progressed toward Charleston it was joined by other traders, White, mixed blood and full blooded Creeks, as well as by a few Cherokees.

One of the traders, a backwoods man from Tennessee, tried to ingratiate himself with Sakoeka and his uncle, Hoponika Futsakia. His attempts were ignored by the Truth Teller until, the second morning after the Tennessee trader had joined the group, Hoponika Futsakia found him untying the thongs holding the pelts and skins on one of Daniel Pearson's pack mules. When the backwoodsman saw that Hoponika Futsakia was coming near the pack animal, he pretended he was adjusting the thongs which he said he noticed had loosened. Since he had already put several pelts and skins on the ground near the pack mule, it was obvious that theft was his object. The following days of the journey, Hoponika Futsakia chose to build his fire and to camp some distance from the others, including the Tennessee trader.

Chagrined at this passive rebuke, the backwoods man at the common camp fire each night regaled the others with tales of his sexual conquests among the Cherokee women of north Georgia and the Carolinas. Most, he said, he seduced easily because they were willing and could see his superiority to their husbands. The virgins were a little harder, but usually he succeeded without rape. As he drank from a bottle of Tennessee moonshine, his voice became louder and more belligerent. Some of the other traders at the campfire laughed and pretended to be impressed with his bragging. Others stirred him to near rage when they expressed some reservations or disbelief. All of this Uriah, Hoponika Futsakia and the Creek/Black, Mabry, could hear distinctly.

Finally, the Tennessee trader, almost too drunk to be cautious, said that his last conquest was a virgin Cherokee who would not give in, and he had had to rape her. Her brothers came for him at the trading post where he was staying and he barely escaped being caught, killed and scalped. For all he knew, they were still on his trail and that was why he had joined this trading party. None of the traders doubted this last confession and he became a pariah for the rest of the trip. When he saw their attitude toward him, he began to doubt that there was safety in the numbers in the party and that he could count on any help in case of a Cherokee attack. His attempts at friendliness were rebuffed by everyone he approached. He finally gave in, resigned himself to being excluded from the group, and hung sulking along the end of the party.

Beginning at the Pitch Tree trading posts, Sakoeka, his uncle and the mix-blooded Creek/Negro, Mabry, had traveled with their horses and pack mules over paths covered by years of pine needles, which, when crushed by horses' hoofs or men's feet let off a clean, pungent odor. All the paths, Indian trails from many years past, were shaded by tall long-leafed pines. A few creeks or branches of small creeks had little water and could be easily crossed, but as the group progressed, creeks became larger and had to be forded, sometimes on horseback, sometimes on foot.

Since the wharves in Charleston were on the end of the peninsula between the Ashley River and the Cooper River at the utmost south-east side of the city, the party took a southern route though Georgia into South Carolina in order to cross the Ashley River as near as possible to the city of Charleston.

Near Charleston, the land changed. Frequently they had to skirt large portions of marshy land hosting what appeared to be fields of palmettos, with a few spindly long-leaf pine trees here and there, often surrounded by large cyprus trees with limbs drooping down to the water and, frequently, centuries old oaks with Spanish moss hanging sometimes almost to the ground. Somewhat later, the marshes turned into swamps which, when possible, the traders crossed on foot, ignoring the water moccasins and alligators which, when disturbed, slithered or swam away. Some of the alligators sunning themselves seemed indifferent to the passers-by, only opening a disinterested eye as they passed. The larger swamps, however, had to be circled on whatever solid ground could be found.

Traveling was much slower than it had been in the high land of upper Georgia and South Carolina. Mosquitoes and gnats plagued White man, and horses alike. The journey through the swamps was punctuated by swatting of gnats and mosquitoes as well as by groans and curses. The mixed breed Muskogee/Whites, Mabry, and the other half blooded Indians as well as the full-blooded Indians seemed to suffer less and to find the pains and irritations of the White men amusing.

The pack mules carrying the goods to be traded as well as food, water, cooking utensils, and Uriah's few clothes and belongings were more sure-footed than were horses and men when crossing the marshes and swamps. More than once some of the traders lost footing, fell, and when upright again were covered with mud, tupelo, rotting vegetation, and algae.

The pack mule which carried Uriah's clothes rubbed against a tree, loosing the leather thongs securing a packet, which, in the middle of a swamp, came loose dumping the packet into the dirty algae and mud. Partially opened, the packet let in water which was not immediately noticed when it was retrieved.

Nearer the Ashley River, giant oaks covered with Spanish moss dotted the landscape, so thick sometimes that they almost shut out light, sunshine, and air. Uriah was fascinated by the variety of fowl, flora and fauna which they met in the swamps and marshes. They saw blue and white herons, white and brown ibis, egrets and ducks. The cat tails and palmettos were sometimes so thick that they seemed a forest. Hawks and vultures circled overhead or sat on dead tree branches. Deer, turkeys, and foxes were glimpsed from time to time. Sweet gum trees were interspersed with cypress trees and cane brakes. Crepe Myrtles flowered pink and bright red on higher ground. Cane rattlers slithered from high ground into underbrush when disturbed.

On the journey of almost two weeks the traders had crossed several small rivers and creeks without difficulty by following the Indian paths where years before the Indians had searched for and found the highest ground and the fewest marshes.

Leaving the boundaries of upper Georgia and entering South Carolina, they traveled southward parallel to the Ashley River and through the Ashley forest on the ancient Muskogee paths in order to cross the river. Inlets and creeks with flood gates let in water to flood large rice fields where slaves and an occasional White overseer labored in the marshy fields, ankle or even calf deep in algae and stinking, rotting vegetation.

Along the Ashley River Road the Indian paths circled or went on the outskirts of Drayton Hall, Middleton Place, and Magnolia Plantation, plantations which had existed before the American Revolution. Such trading parties were seen frequently along the ancient paths and, skirting the main quarters, they were seldom noticed and attracted little attention. The big houses could be glimpsed from the paths from time to time and the spacious grounds surrounding them were marvels to Uriah. Some outbuildings were slave quarters, while others were kitchens as well as sheds for household and farm supplies.

Women outside the slave houses, glimpsed from afar, were weaving sweet grass baskets, tending children, or working in small kitchen gardens. Some slave houses were made for two families and handmade bricks made them more permanent and warmer than the stick and mud houses of Uriah's village. Both black slaves and White men paid little heed to the party skirting the rice fields where slaves and overseers alike endured the humidity, oppressive heat, mosquitoes, and the stench from the rotting vegetation in the water used to flood the rice fields.

Since Uriah's uncle's party was a large one and consisted of men, pack mules and horses, it was necessary to make several trips to cross the Ashley River by ferry. Most of the traders found the loss of time in having to take several ferry loads across the river a source of irritation.

On the eastern side of the Ashley River, the signs of the White man's civilization became primary. The marshes seemed to have a utilitarian purpose. The first settlement entered, the village of Islington, only sparsely covered by houses, used the ebb and flow of the tides to power lumber mills. Very near the river were large mill ponds, some stagnant and filled with debris and algae, some only recently filled.

Sakoeka's uncle, Hoponika Futsakia, the Truth Teller, decided to quit the rest of the party and remain at a small rough inn on the outskirts of the first village of any size in order to rest both humans as well as horses and mules before continuing the journey to the Charleston wharves and business district where he was to meet John Pearson and turn over to him Sokoeka/Uriah, the nephew of both.

Mabry, the Creek/Negro, had relatives in the vicinity and left to visit them, promising to return early, before sun-up, the next day. The Tennessee backwoods man also quit the party on the entry into the outskirts of the village.

When Hoponika Futsakia went to see to the animals, Uriah decided to try on his White man's clothes so as to enter Charleston as the son of his Irish father. However, when he untied the packet containing his trousers, shirt and shoes and tried to put them on, he found that he could not quite button his trousers and that they were several inches too short. This was the result of a sudden spurt of growth since he had last put them on and of the shrinkage due to the moisture which entered when the packet was dumped in the swamp. There was also a distinctly bad odor from both the packet and the clothing.

As Uriah was pondering what to do about his problems, the Tennessee backwoods man entered and immediately began guffawing, "Look at the little Indian boy playin' like he's a White boy. Com'ere little make-believe White boy and let's see whatcha look like without Indian britches."

He grabbed Uriah around the neck from the back and began with his free hand to try to pull off Uriah's trousers. While Uriah was fighting, struggling, and screaming, his uncle entered. He, in his turn, grabbed the Tennessean from the back around the neck and squeezed. The backwoods man released his hold on Uriah and Uriah dropped to the floor at his feet. Without releasing Uriah's attacker, Hoponika Futsakia turned him around to face him. "For this, by Muskogee law, you deserve death, but we're in the White man's territory. Here the law says it's no crime to kill a Muskogee, but it's a crime for a Muskogee to kill a White man. If I kill you here, the White man's law will punish both me and my nephew. I'll not kill you here and now. But, pay me attention! Know that in Muskogee territory, it's not a crime for a Muskogee to kill a White man or another Muskogee for good cause. What you've just tried to do is good cause, and if you come into Creek territory, you'll be killed, either by me, by my brothers in our clan, or by this boy is he's old enough. So that you'll remember this and so we may recognize you if you come, I'll take a piece of your skin from your arm just here."

He drew his knife and took a piece of skin from the Tennessee backwoods man's upper arm on the fleshy part of the arm, on the outside, just under the joint of the arm and shoulder. When the Tennessean screamed and struggled, Hoponika Futsakia released him after taking a thin four-inch strip of flesh.

"If you want to tell the White men what I did, do so. You'll also have to tell them why I did it, and I don't think you will."

He shoved the bleeding, groaning and cursing Tennessean towards the door. This done, he turned back into the room. For him, the incident was closed. The backwoodsman had been warned and marked. The choice of life or death was up to him.

For Uriah the attack had been a shock and a revelation. Born into the Wind Clan, the highest clan of the Muskogees, brought up by two strong uncles, living with a doting mother and a father richer than anyone else in the Pitch Tree area, until this day he had no idea but that he was the center of everyone's universe. That anyone could manhandle him and attempt sodomy or rape would never have entered his mind. How to live with this revelation and how to protect himself in the future preoccupied him.

But his uncle seemed not to notice Uriah's fears. "There's a path down to the river. We need to wash the mud and smell from the swamp off our bodies. Don't worry about your White man's clothes. Your uncle John will have others made which fit you when we meet him in Charleston."

He led the way to the river where they both rubbed sand from the river bank on their bodies to remove body oil, dirt, mud, and the swamp stench and afterwards swam for half an hour. Returning to the inn they saw no sign of the backwoodsman. The inn was not clean; temporary rooms were provided by dividing each by dirty homespun cloth slung on a rope. Because the sheets for the beds were equally dirty. Uriah and Hoponika Futsakia made beds of deer skin on the floor.

The Truth Teller slept soundly but Uriah still tried to resolve his problem. He wanted to please his father and try to live for a while in a world his father had known. He was also lured by the mystery of what was in that world and whether he would like it. On the other hand, he wondered, "What if another White man tries the same thing the Tennessean did? Truth Teller will be back in our village. Without him, in a country I don't know and not knowing enough English, I couldn't protect myself. And if I tried, and if I killed the next man, wouldn't I be punished by the White man's law and killed? No, I'm not ready for the White man's world. I'll have to explain that to Truth Teller."

Eva, who told this story, said she would never have known these things if she had not lived with her grandfather until she was married. He had kept the correspondence of Daniel Pearson, her great-grandfather, with his brother, John, as well as records from the trading posts and John's early life in Charleston, as well as John's wife's diaries and such newspapers from the north as they had chanced to have.

As events turned out, he was grateful both to them and to Truth Teller that he had a record of the events which he could only half remember as he grew older. At the time, however, he said that he, fearing what would happen to him, unprotected, in the White man's world, changed his mind and told Truth Teller the following morning that he would not be staying in Charleston, but that he would like, nevertheless, to meet his uncle John and after he had done that he would return with him to the Muskogee at the Pitch Tree settlement when he had finished Daniel Pearson's business in Charleston.

Truth Teller listened until he had finished and then answered shortly, "No, your life cannot be lived by what might be. Your word to Daniel must be kept. You'll stay."

Mabry, the Creek/Negro, had said that he would meet them at the village inn at daybreak, after spending the night with his father's people outside the village. However, two hours after sunup he still had not arrived. At about 9:00 o'clock he arrived explaining the reasons for his delay. Leaving his relations, freed Negroes, he had been stopped by a group of White men. These claimed to believe that he was a run-away slave.

Even after he produced the documentation stating his freed status and the commission from Daniel introducing him to John Pearson and to various merchants in Charleston, they still detained him. One or two wanted to destroy his papers and take him to the authorities to claim the reward for runaway slaves. Most of them, however, were afraid that, if his story was true, he had too many contacts among the Whites, Daniel Pearson in the Pitch Tree Settlement and John Pearson in Charleston, for such a ruse to be safe. Their arguments and wrangling took several hours, but at the end they released him with his documentation intact.

Leaving the sparsely settled village of Islington, Mabry, Uriah and Truth Teller followed the Ashley River through Ashley forest a short distance toward Charleston. Hoponika Futsakia had decided to cross part of the peninsula by way of Broad Street to King Street and then south to the wharves to be able to arrive near the Cooper River side of Charleston. Near the river, on the outskirts of the city, the land was marshy and frequently cut by small creeks.

As they neared the residential area of the city, however, sturdy, elegant houses of stone and brick built by British trained architects 50 or some 100 years earlier appeared on the highest ground. These were wonders to Uriah, who had up to this time seen only Muskogee houses, log cabins and, from a distance, several plantation houses. A number of these elegant houses, with smaller houses for carriages, for kitchens, and for slave house servants, together formed a small growing village.

When Uriah was told this was not yet Charleston proper, he was astonished because he could not believe anything could be greater than these several grand houses.

Both Hoponika Futsakia and Mabry, who had delivered skins and pelts to Charleston merchants several times, explained that there was no need to spend much time in the center of Charleston, since the coastal wharves where merchants had shops were their destinations.

Daniel's brother, John, would most likely take Uriah to shops in the more fashionable districts once their business with merchants, whose shops and sometimes their houses, were near the waterfront, was completed and they were free of the burden of skins, pelts, and pack mules.

Nevertheless, Hoponika Futsakia took a longer route to the wharves than was his custom so as to impress Uriah with the size and wealth of even the suburbs of Charleston. They entered Broad Street from the Ashley River and as they progressed eastward, the houses, and businesses became larger and the traffic of carts, mules, horses, carriages and people became greater. Houses of two and three or four stories made of stone, brick or dressed lumber painted in various colors, sometimes with shutters painted in matching or contrasting colors and occasionally with stone, brick or wrought iron fences surrounding them showed clearly the wealth and importance of the owners. Some of the larger mansions had outbuildings in addition to those for cooking and houses for slaves, extensive gardens at the rear of the house with carefully tended plants and trees and an occasional fountain, making them appear almost as separate villages in themselves.

Midway they turned into King Street, named for King George I, to go south to the east side of the peninsula to Bay and Battery Streets where they were to meet John Pearson at the shop of a merchant who lived above his business so as to be available to ships which docked and departed night and day.

Uriah had never seen ships, large bodies of water or so many busy, hurrying Whites. The wharves stretched as far along the waterfront as he could see. Every foot of the wharves was covered by shops, houses, fish mongers, equipment for sea-going vessels and sailors from both the former colonies and from Britain.

Ships newly arrived were unloading goods from many parts of the world. Custom agents were dealing with masters of vessels concerning import duties owed to the State and to the City of Charleston. Ships being readied for departure were loading cotton, indigo, and rice. One ship was unloading its cargo of slaves newly arrived from the islands in the West Indies, some of whom, the old, the very young and the sick, had already been let off at Sullivan's Island, directly across from the wharves. Those already off the vessel on the wharf in Charleston were waiting to be transported to the Slave Market for sale to plantation owners as well as to private individuals in Charleston who wanted to buy slaves for use in the large mansions in the city.

There was a smell from the newly arrived slaves which was more than unwashed human bodies. The slaves had spent several weeks in the hold of a slave ship, sometimes with fecal matter, urine, and sometimes dead and rotting bodies. In addition to these smells, there was a smell which blended them all and the best Sakoeka/Uriah could identify it was as something that approached the overwhelming odor of fear.

At one of larger shops midway down the street lining the waterfront, they stopped before an imposing dwelling with glass windows on which a sign indicated that the owner would buy and ship articles, particularly animal skins and pelts, rice and indigo. A servant came out and indicated that they were to enter from the side of the building where there was provision for unloading the pack animals. They did as instructed and then entered the shop to find John Pearson awaiting them.

John Pearson did not bear much resemblance to his brother Daniel. Daniel was tall, slim, brunet and very serious, whereas John was somewhat shorter, with brown curly hair and very blue eyes which laughed at the whole world. When he saw the group he had been expecting, he laughed with genuine good humor. "Well, there you are. I've been here all this day waiting for you. I'm very glad to see you all safely arrived, but let me look at my famous nephew. "

Examining Uriah he summed up his opinion, "My boy, you look like your father at your age. Irish you are, but the Creek in you, I have no doubt, is hidden somewhere inside."

He hugged Uriah and shook his hand. "I'm very glad to see you and much obliged to my brother for sending me such a handsome fellow.""

Uriah/Sakoeka said he was surprised and embarrassed by his uncle John's behavior. His Creek relatives rarely touched and almost never embraced. Staring at his uncle he used his limited English to say he too was glad to be in Charleston, but privately within his own mind he reserved his judgment for further acquaintance.

The wharves were extensive and filled with many varieties of humanity. Sailors, dock hands and customs agents mingled, talking or arguing. The smell was one of the first impressions Uriah had of the White man's commerce and the impression was not favorable. Fishermen were unloading tons of fish which were being bought by fish mongers and by eating establishments both on the waterfront and in the city of Charleston.

The smell for one from the inland was not inviting. Unwashed sailors and dock hands smelled almost as repugnant as the newly arrived slaves. In addition to these odors, refuse which had accumulated on the docks had not been disposed of regularly. Rotting and disintegrating hemp bags which had formerly held rice or indigo were stacked against buildings near new and less odorous cargo waiting to be loaded.

Uriah's reactions to the smells and dock scenes were as divided as his heritage. On the one hand, he admired the tall ships with their spars rising to the sky and the wealth and activity which the wharves represented. On the other hand, he contrasted the chaos, dirt and refuse with the orderliness, cleanliness and respect for nature which his small village represented.

His Uncle John interrupted his observations. "I have to make several stops here on the wharves on business matters before we settle in. There are some peddler's carts on almost all the wharves. They have boiled corn, corn bread, and usually some gumbo. I've already eaten. The three of you can eat while I finish some commissions I have near here."

John Pearson's comment hid the fact that none of the three would have been allowed in regular establishments where they might have sat at a table to eat. Uriah's clothing identified him as a non-white as did both the clothing and skin color of Truth Teller and Mabry, and as such much in White Charleston was closed to them.

When John Pearson mentioned his commissions, Mabry and Hoponika Fustakia looked at each other but did not say anything. They knew, and Uriah was to find out, that John Pearson's commission was to a merchant at the far end of the harborside whose three shops extended outward almost to reach the wharf. The merchant, a Scots immigrant named George McGown, lived in the upper story of the largest of the shops. John Pearson had been trying to court Lucinda, the only daughter of that merchant, for the better part of two years. The merchant did not approve of his suit and they had had what was supposed to be a definitive conversation concerning the matter almost a year before at John's last visit. The merchant had explained his position clearly.

"John, you and I are merchants. We like what we do and are not ashamed of it. We both have made money and we intend to make more. I now have three shops here near the wharves and I've recently bought five thousand acres outside of town. I have an overseer and slaves clearing the land. They'll plant rice and indigo at the next season. You don't approve of slavery. My daughter has never been without slaves as servants. Her dead mother and I agreed that our daughter would be raised as a lady and would be one if we could manage it. Lucinda does not cook, clean or do anything else a slave can do for her. Her only accomplishments are fine needle work and teacup painting. What would she do in your wilderness? How would she fit in at your trading post? No, it will never do. You must surely see that."

John Pearson agreed with much of what McGowan had said, but he countered with, "What you say is mostly true, but it seems to me the matter is between Lucinda and me. If she is willing to marry me and try our luck together in what you call my wilderness, then she can take a Negro maid and a cook with her. They will be her slaves and not mine. She won't have to do any more menial work in the wilderness than she does here. The accommodations there will not be as fashionable or luxurious as here, but she won't be uncomfortable."

McGowan's position did not change. "John, her looks and my money will attract, and are now attracting suitors enough. Go back to your wilderness and find some girl more suited to the life there. She will forget you in time. If you want to marry her, I'd have no objection to a son-in-law like you who bought the shop down the wharf which will be for sale next year. The owner is old and intends to go live with his daughter in Savannah. You can see the advantage to that proposition for all three of us. Think it over and let me know when you come back next year."

Angry and with wounded pride, John Pearson had returned to his trading post and when he had corresponded with Daniel Pearson he had intended to return to Charleston one last time and put his affairs there in the hands of an intermediary who would come to the trading post and return to Charleston to sell to or barter with whoever would give the best price. He intended at that time never to return to Charleston after he had established Uriah in his school. His object when he left Uriah and his party on the wharves was to ask Lucinda to make a decision, either to agree with her father and stay in Charleston or to try her life with him at the trading post. If she agreed with her father his decision was to say goodbye to Lucinda and wish her well.

When he arrived at the living quarters above the main shop and was admitted by the Negro maid, he found himself only one of three callers. The other two were young gentlemen of Charleston, both quite handsome and fashionably dressed. Their manners were extremely civilized, although beneath the surface of the words he sensed some disdain for his tanned face and the clothes he had traveled in. Lucinda blushed when she saw him, but she too was very cordial and seemed glad to see him. John's resolve began to weaken. George McGowan, he saw, knew whereof he spoke. Lucinda would not be without suitors enough. Perhaps she would forget him soon. But, judging by their conversation, he wondered if Lucinda could see that they were as much interested in her father's wealth as with her good looks. He left somewhat abruptly and before the first of the two young gentlemen.He had recognized one of the two callers whom he knew by sight as being the younger son of a major plantation owner outside of Charleston. Since most of the plantation owners with roots in Britain kept the English aristocratic custom of entailment, this younger son would inherit none of his father's plantation acreage nor house. Both would go intact to his elder brother. He would be expected to find his livelihood elsewhere. His usual choices were the clergy, the military, or marriage. He had obviously chosen to begin working on the last alternative. Although John had arrived determined, if Lucinda agreed with her father, to end his courtship and to return to his trading post without the encumbrance of a wife or fiancée, he felt robbed and cheated of something that belonged to him by right, not of birth but of merit. He would make a better husband for Lucinda than this young fashion plate who had birth, good manners and good looks, but nothing else more valuable and enduring.

By the time he had returned to the wharf where he had left Uriah, Mabry, and Hoponika Futsakia, his anger has worn off and logic had taken its place. He would at least confer with the merchant at the end of McGowan's wharf. If the terms were satisfactory, he might stay a while in Charleston as a merchant.

Since it was too late to go back to downtown Charleston to outfit Uriah, he said that they would finish selling their skins and pelts. Afterwards they would visit another friend of his who would be glad to have them as guests for the night.

Uriah was bored with the bargaining necessary to get the best price. He would have liked to have gone aboard one of the ships anchored in the harbor, but John warned him that the British sometimes shanghaied young men, both from the harbors and shores of the former British colonies as well as from United States' ships at sea. The British had lost many men during their long war with the French and were not particularly careful where they found replacements. Although the United States government protested, in general they were ineffectual and any man taken was likely to remain a prisoner toiling in the service of his Majesty's maritime, or die from overwork and disease.

Hoponika Futsakia and Mabry declined the invitation to spend the night with Uriah and John at John's friend's house, saying that when they finished selling Daniel's merchandise they had other commissions for him, since they would return to the trading post with cloth, rice, and other necessities which the trading post sold or which Daniel's family there needed. After they had finished they would get a start on the return trip before daybreak.

When they had left, John Pearson decided that it would be best to buy Uriah some temporary shoes and clothes at shops on the waterfront. The following day they would go into Charleston to a tailor located near Ropemakers Street to outfit him for the long months ahead when he would be in school. He decided that he too would be outfitted as a Charleston gentleman.

John's decision to have himself made a suit of elegant city clothes had a two-fold reason. First of all, he thought it prudent to accompany Uriah in his first encounter with a Charleston tailor, and in the next place, he would need such a suit if turned out that he was to be married in Charleston. And for the second eventuality, he thought it best to settle first with Lucinda's father to see if his approval still held and then with Lucinda to discuss their mutual family concerns, and then to contract with the old merchant who owned the shop adjacent to the last of George McGowan's shops.

When Lucinda's father heard that John was willing to consider taking his advice and remain in Charleston, as the nearest merchant to his own shops, he was both happy and ready to be generous, for in truth he was of the same opinion concerning Lucinda's gentleman suitors as was John, although he would have accepted either of them, but less willingly.

"My boy, my son," he said, "I've always thought you the best of the lot and I want you to be happy with your bargain. If Lucinda agrees, as you think she will, I'm prepared to lend you whatever you need to start your business here. If you want to keep your trading post also, I'll understand, and I think it would probably be prudent to do so. If the British invade, as some say they will, we may all need a place inland. My quarters above the central shop are large and already have household servants. There is enough room there for you and Lucinda and me. As soon as I have a house built on the plantation, I'll move there—two, three, four years at the most. You don't have to give me an answer right off. You'd better go now and close with Lucinda, or all of our talk may come to nothing."

When John took Uriah with him to call on Lucinda, he quickly introduced him as his nephew and saw no negative reaction. That done, he moved to a window with Lucinda where he made short work of his proposal.

She showed no surprise. “Of course, John,” she said gently. “Why did you wait so long to ask? We’ll live wherever you choose, in Charleston, or at your trading post. It doesn’t matter to me, so long as you are satisfied with the arrangement. I’m not so fragile as my father seems to think. The thought of going with you into your wilderness gives me no fear or apprehension.”

John, himself, on the other hand, had been somewhat apprehensive, but for a different reason, although he hid the fact. He was anticipating a negative reaction of those in Charleston to his Creek relatives, but he should not have been. Some second, or third, generation mixed-blood Muskogees held high positions in Georgia and the Carolinas, or were nearly related to those who did.

Ultimately, the Governor of Georgia himself, a White, was first cousin to the mixed-blood, William McIntosh, head of the Lower Creeks in Coweta Village. If there was prejudice at the moment Uriah met John’s future in-laws, it was on Uriah’s part. He thought Lucinda’s father wrong in his attempt to decide his daughter’s fate in marriage and a man too concerned with money, although he agreed that his uncle John was a more suitable bridegroom.

Having secured both George McGowan’s and Lucinda’s agreement to his marriage, John lost no time taking Uriah with him to visit the owner of the shop which was reportedly to be for sale. The owner was a Russian Jewish emigrant, Abraham Rouglin, who had begun his life as a peddler in Charleston, which had the largest Jewish population of any city in the Continental United States during the 18th and 19th centuries. Rouglin had quickly established himself as a merchant and built a shop on the wharf with an apartment over it. His family had grown up there. His wife was dead and one of his two daughters was already married to a merchant in Savannah and the other, whose husband was also a merchant, was in the process of establishing her family there also.

Abraham Rouglin intended to sell his business and accompany his younger daughter and her family to Savannah. When John and Uriah met him, he had already been told of John's intentions by George McGowan. They talked terms and price. John said he would have to contact the Bank of the United States for a loan to cover part of the price. However, Abraham said he was willing to let him pay in installments, with no interest, the balance of whatever he could not cover in cash. In addition, he said he had already established himself with his daughter's family in the city and had closed down his own living quarters and sold his slaves. He said that John could move in immediately, that evening even. He was a man of some sensitivity as well as candor.

"I know you can stay with your future father-in-law, but before your marriage that may be somewhat delicate. But do not let me persuade you if you prefer to make other arrangements."

John was more relieved than he liked to show. George McGowan's offer to share his own housing had not pleased him, for he felt he would be starting his married life indebted to him and, since McGowan's personality was as strong as his own, conflicts might arise if they shared living arrangements. He and Uriah were only too glad to accept and thereby had no need to seek other shelter. John was pleased in being thus near Lucinda and Uriah was pleased in being near the activity of the wharves and in sight of the ships arriving and departing.

From pride, not shyness, Uriah had spoken little. Having been assured by his father that he spoke English poorly through his own laziness or negligence, he did not want to run the risk of embarrassment or of having to be grateful to the Whites for their forbearance or kindness because of his inadequate command of English. However, he found Lucinda almost a Muskogee in straight forwardness and felt she would neither pity him nor excuse his mistakes. So, when John suggested including her in the visit to the tailor, Uriah did not object.

John intended to make the trip an occasion for both Uriah and Lucinda. Although Lucinda had been born in Charleston and had lived there all her life, as an only child and the daughter of a merchant, she had not been included in the social life of Charleston. The young men of her acquaintance had met her through her father's business. And, although her father had social aspirations, he had not had time from his growing businesses to find a way into Charleston society.

She was aware that her Charleston suitors were willing to overlook her antecedents and their embarrassment of her merchant father because of the wealth she would inherit. However, although elegant Charleston society was in 1811 difficult to enter, even by marriage, the grandfathers of those who now had summer houses in the city to take advantage of the sea breezes, and winter plantation houses in the country, had at first grubbed for a living.

Immigrants fleeing persecution as Huguenots, or Scots and Irish fleeing degradation and poverty, they had felled trees, planted rice fields, built and manned flood gates for rice fields along with their slaves. Their sons had expanded on their work in ways requiring less physical labor. They had entered not only trade, but acquired additional slaves and real estate and dealt both in the slave trade and in money lending. The second generation had frequently upwards of 500 slaves and managed at least 40,000 acres

The present generation, the great-grandsons, to which her suitors belonged, frequently returned to the Europe their great-grandfathers had left in poverty or relative poverty, but returned there as wealthy men. After a grand tour of Europe, they frequently married into wealthy English families or studied law at the Temple Bar. Others studied architecture and as gentlemen architects, once home, designed and furnished mansions for themselves or their relatives.

They pretended to forget their origins and took on aristocratic airs. Lucinda had no such pretensions and no such aspirations. She had never been ashamed of the fact that her antecedents on both sides of her family had for a long time been "measurers of yards and tiers of packets." That she and John would continue as merchants seemed to her to be comfortable and suitable.

Lucinda's mother, before she died, had given her basic instruction in letters and numbers, as well as in sewing, embroidery, and fancy needlework. Her father had hired tutors for Lucinda for music, painting, dancing, and for a little English literature and French. These, he thought, would, when the time came, see her through whatever Charleston society had to offer or required.

Although he wanted to enter Charleston society for the sake of his daughter, George McGowan was no more deceived than was his daughter concerning the origins of many of the city's aristocrats. The French man of letters and New York farmer, de Toqueville, when in Charleston in the last century had written of the city at that time,

"The inhabitants are the gayest in America; it is called the centre of our beau monde and is always filled with the richest planters of the province, who resort hither in quest of health and pleasure...The round of pleasure, and expenses of these citizens' tables, are much superior to what you would imagine; indeed, the growth of this town and province has been astonishingly rapid...."

Later, in the next century, when Charleston had grown to become the fourth largest city in the United States and the third largest seaport, visitors wrote, much to McGowan's amusement, that Charleston's merchants were opulent, well-bred and the richest in the United States. They also said that for grandeur, splendor of buildings, decorations, equipages, numbers, commerce and shipping, Charleston rivaled many European cities.

John found Abraham's quarters more than adequate. Uriah found them luxurious. They spent a comfortable night there and, since there were no servants, they ate breakfast on the wharf and then went to find a livery stable. John wanted to impress Lucinda and Uriah and hired both a surrey and a driver. John Pearson was vain enough and young enough to enjoy showing off his learning to impress Lucinda. He explained that some of the cobblestone streets were paved with stones from Great Britain which came off cargo ships as ballast. When discarded, they were retrieved to provide solid, long enduring streets. The areas around the Exchange and Custom House were not exceptionally impressive, but adjacent streets provided elegance enough, but even these were overshadowed by other streets as they wound their way through Charleston and its suburbs.

The shortest route was not important, since John intended to profit by the occasion to spend a whole day with Lucinda. In a leisurely drive, they covered Legare Street, Meeting Street, Rutledge Avenue, South Battery Street, and completed their day ultimately at Tradd Street.

The elegant houses and spacious grounds did not impress Lucinda, who had seen them many times and had no desire to be invited to enter them, but in order not to disappoint John she pretended enthusiasm.

Uriah, seeing such wealth and grandeur for the fist time, had a divided reaction. There was real enthusiasm and excitement during the tour, although hidden under his Muskogee impassive exterior. But his Muskogee past could not reconcile such private wealth reserved in a large house for only one family. He contrasted the cultivated perfection of the gardens with the natural setting of his village where nature was tampered with as little as possible and where all, men, women, young and old shared everything and none were forgotten after the harvest. However, on the tour, whatever his reservations about the White man, Legare Street was his favorite. He could not stay long enough looking at the mansions and gardens of Legare Street. Most of the dwellings were almost estates, holding outbuildings used as kitchens, wash rooms, carriage houses and slave quarters, the whole surrounded by extensive, well-kept gardens which ensured privacy and beauty.

The outing into Charleston's neighborhoods was followed by a visit in the mid-afternoon to a tailor near Rope Makers Alley John Pearson had heard of. He was reputed to be the best in Charleston. John was to buy only one city suit, and this for his wedding.

Uriah, however, needed clothes enough for several months. The first would be a city suit for John and Lucinda's wedding if the school allowed him to attend, but the others would be school clothes, neither too simple nor too elegant. Since this tailor outfitted many young men of South Carolina for school, they relied on his judgment and settled on commissioning seven complete outfits and the city suit, as well as a few additional shirts. The complete outfits included under garments. These, which Uriah had never worn, nor had he seen the use for, he at first objected to. The White man, he thought, made everything complicated, even those things which should have been very simple.

The tailor was of a garrulous nature. As tailor to ships' captains, plantation owners, and wealthy merchants, he heard and passed on gossip as well as new information from northern states as well as from France and Great Britain.

John Pearson profited by the time it took to choose fabric for himself and Uriah and to undergo various measurements to find out the latest information about the status of what was said to be a pending war between the former Colonies, now the United States of America, and Great Britain.

To encourage the tailor to begin reciting facts and gossip, John said, "If there is war, it will hinder my sending money back to Ireland. I don't know how they'll get by without it. My brother, this boy's father, and I have been sending our family there money by way of a captain we've known for some time. Do you think there's anything to the rumors we hear about an invasion? Will there be war, do you think, between the United States and Great Britain again?"

No question could have been more welcome to the tailor. The day before and that very morning also, he had taken measurements for two captains, one from New England and one newly arrived from a circuitous route to French ports, which were supposedly closed because of France's Berlin and Milan decrees. The first had left a Boston newspaper, some weeks old to be sure, but still interesting. The Boston newspaper was complaining that President Jefferson's policies, beginning with the embargo, were ruining New England shipping. The same complaint, coupled with threats of secession by the New England states, had been frequently reported in Boston newspapers for several years. Massachusetts lawmakers reiterated that all the states, Massachusetts in particular, were sovereign states which had granted only limited powers to the Federal government. The Embargo which had been in effect for several years was by 1811 revoked, but the damage to shipping had already been done. The article in the Boston newspaper maintained that the Embargo had from the beginning been unconstitutional, that no one had been obligated to obey it, and that Massachusetts was, in most respects, still a sovereign and independent state. The Boston sea captain reported that New England shippers and the public of those states were ready to secede from the Union if the President could not make more progress in protecting shipping. Another Boston newspaper had reported that "It is better to suffer the amputation of a limb, (meaning the severance of New England from the Union), than to lose the whole body. We must prepare for the operation."

He also said that one of his friends, who worked for a Boston newspaper, had heard it reported that Mr. Jefferson had said that as bad as the results of the Embargo were, the people would have to choose, either the Embargo or war with England.

The other captain, the one of the morning visit newly arrived from docking at various French ports, had regaled the tailor with a story current in France about Napoleon's reaction to the American ambassador to France. He reported that the story there was that Napoleon was incensed that the American ambassador could not speak French and that he wrote four-line letters on matters of grave importance which deserved more time and more French. It was said that he told his ambassador, the Duke de Cadore, "Write to America in such manner that the President may know what a fool has been sent here."

The tailor interrupted himself, "Haven't you heard most of these things? You have, you say, come to Charleston once a year for several years. You've seen, of course, that during the Embargo Charleston suffered very little. Everything here is less hurried and less strict than in New England. We've always had captains who were not too concerned about what flag they flew where and when. The only time our harbor was blockaded it was not by a European power but by Black Beard, the pirate. Some of the captains are British subjects working for Charleston merchants. They found then and still find ways in and out of the Charleston harbor as well as ways in and out of British and French ports. Their difficulties doing so made and do make goods more expensive and raise the cost of doing business, but still the increase in cost has not been beyond reason."

John answered that he had heard of the Embargo, but that he had not noticed any scarcity of the kinds of goods his trading post sold, although he had noticed at the last several visits that the prices were somewhat elevated. As for a pending war with England, that he had not heard of back in his wilderness, although, he supposed it was to be expected. In addition to the complaints about the British interfering with shipping and taking American sailors off American ships on the high seas, there had always been talk by Southerners of invading and annexing Canada and chasing the British out of the American continent once and for all.

John Pearson had been congratulating himself for more than twenty-four hours on his good fortune: Lucinda had agreed to marry him; the merchant Rouglin had agreed to sell him his store and inventory; and he could keep his trading post. Now, after this short visit to the tailor he had second thoughts. "If there is war, there is no way to tell how long it will last. The British, who control the high seas, would assuredly blockade all American ports. Without goods to sell I wouldn't be able to meet my commitments to the merchant Rouglin. My married life would start off with more difficulties and debt than even I can imagine."

Sunk in his own unpleasant thoughts on the way back to the waterfront and to Lucinda's father's stores, he did not notice that Uriah was talking, jabbering even, to Lucinda and making a mistake about every tenth word in either grammar or pronunciation. Lucinda had corrected him for a few minutes and then, laughing, but not offending Uriah, she said she would have to have a rest and would correct only ten percent of his errors. At that they both laughed and began to notice John, whose recent happiness had been disrupted by the visit to the tailor.

The gossip about a pending war with England changed all his recently made plans. Blockade of all ports, American, English, and French, as well as of the ports of their possessions, would mean paying a high price to blockade runners and incurring the risk of total loss, by theft or capture by the British on the high seas. The economy would in fact be shut down, as had happened with New England shipping during the recent

Embargo imposed by President Jefferson. Many businesses in New England had been ruined, apparently not to recover. John was pondering which visit he should make first, that to the merchant Rouglin, to Lucinda's father, or to the captain who had been delivering mail to his parents in Ireland by a circuitous route.

By the time they reached Lucinda's father's stores he had decided that a visit to the captain would be the logical first step. First he must verify the tailor's information, then he would decide how to approach Rouglin and McGowan.

He easily located the captain the next day, but his visit with him did not quell his fears. The captain assured him that all merchant ships were in danger from English man of warships, with or without a declared war. Any American ship within range of a British warship could be chased down, boarded and the crew subjected to a search for able-bodied seamen. It was always the youngest, healthiest and most able-bodied they took, saying they were deserters from the English navy. These would be taken on board the English ship in spite of the protests of the American captain and in spite of any documentation presented to show American citizenship. Diplomatic protests against such impressments produced no results. Both for this reason and for the fact that some men in power were urging the immediate invasion and annexation of Canada to complete what they considered the logical conclusion of the War for Independence, the feeling among the merchant captains was that war was not only inevitable but imminent.

This information confirmed John's intention to try to annul his recent commitments. He decided to attack George McGowan first with all the reasons why he should marry Lucinda and take her into the interior. The trading station would be sufficiently far from the coast to make threat of war there less likely.

McGowan listened to his reasons but was unimpressed and unmoved. "Yes, there will very likely be a blockade of Charleston and other southern ports, as well as a blockade of all New England ports. However, the danger will be greater in New England where ports are more numerous and closer together. The Southern ports are fewer and farther apart. Only Charleston, Savannah, and New Orleans on the Gulf Coast have any commercial significance. To blockade all these would mean spreading the British fleet too thin. A second reason for discounting the importance of a British blockade is that, during the recent Embargo, Charleston and Savannah captains succeeded in running the blockade by various stratagems. The experience they gained ought to be very valuable and useful during a war period. A third reason, which you ought to understand, as a business man, John, is that during the Embargo and after, Charleston merchants who could afford to do so, increased their inventory of imported durable goods, particularly furniture, cloth, and farm implements. Merchants with storage space, such as my houses and Rouglin's have a back inventory for at least a year or more without depending too much on blockade runners."

His fourth and most compelling reason was that the American navy was infinitely insignificant in comparison to that of the English, who commanded the sea in all parts of the world they chose to sail in. That fact meant that, in the event of a declared war, the Americans would have to depend mainly on private vessels which would be commissioned by the Federal government to search for and destroy English ships. These privateers, which in peace time would be considered pirates, could legitimately take booty from any British ship they could board and overcome. The privateers sailed ships lighter and faster than the heavy man-of-war or the loaded commercial vessels of the English. Charleston merchants, himself included, were now opening communications with owners of private ships to form a consortium if privateers were commissioned by the Federal government in the event of war. The shared booty in any privateer in which they had an interest should more than make up for any commercial loss due to the blockade.

McGowan's reasons opened a new world of activities to John Pearson, who had until then no idea of this sort of commerce. He wondered how the United States Government could justify this type of piracy and then he wondered if the merchant Rouglin had laid up a year's supplies in the large upper story of his business. The answer to that question would, he decided, make a decision for him. If Rouglin's inventory included goods for the rest of 1811 and all of 1812, that would give him time in the event of war to make further decisions. He could always return to the trading post.

Chapter III

Fall 1811

The merchant Rouglin's inventory proved, according to the merchant and verified by John Pearson, to be at least sufficient for a year and a half, and perhaps more.

And so John Pearson's fate and that of Uriah/Sakoeka Pearson was decided on the basis of the inventory of the Russian immigrant Rouglin. Nothing remained for John Pearson to do before beginning his new life in Charleston but to take Uriah to his new school.

That journey he started on the following day. The two-day ride gave Uriah a chance to become acquainted with his uncle as well as an opportunity to explain his life in the Pitch Tree Settlement. What he told John was not great news to his uncle, since John Pearson had been living among the Cherokees for more years than Uriah/Sakoeka had been alive. This did not occur to Uriah/Sakoeka, who thought his uncle needed educating in the ways of the Muskogees.

He first told John about his uncles, saying he and his younger uncle were almost the same age and that they did not agree with his father and Truth Teller, his older uncle, that the Muskogee should wait before joining either the English or the Americans.

"My father isn't a Muskogee and he doesn't really understand the obligations of a Creek, especially a man of the Wind Clan, although he says he does. I have obligations to my mother and my sisters. I must be there to protect them. My father and my uncles may not always be there to help. I must help my clan protect the land. We cannot live without protecting the forest which feeds the animals we need for food and clothing and the open land we need for farming. If the White man destroys the woods and trees we will lose also the roots, plants and berries our women use to prepare medicine. My mother and my uncles tell me I must also continue to protect the graves of the ancestors, whose spirits protect and guide us."

Truth Teller had taken him to the council meeting to hear the great Tecumseh, whose mother, Methoataske, was a Creek and his father, Puckeshinwa, a Shawnee. Tecumseh had come from the North to visit all the southern tribes, leaving his brother, The Prophet, to care for the tribes there. He and his younger uncle agreed with Tecumseh that all tribes from the Hurons, the Delawares, the Wyanadottes, the Kikapoos, Pottawatomies, the Winnebagoes, the Ottawawas, the Chippawas, the Sacs, the Miamies, and the Shawnees in the north to the Creeks, the Cherokees, the Choctaws, the Chickasaws and the Seminoles in Florida in the south should unite to oppose the White man who gobbled up more and more of their territory every year. The White man destroyed the forest and drove away or killed the game, depriving the tribes not only of food, but of clothing and medicine which came from the forest or the creatures of the forest. Only through uniting could the tribes hope to retain their land and life.

He said that both he and his uncle had found the Great Tecumseh a man of truth. He spoke only about the needs of the Indian, and never of himself.

Uriah told his grand-daughter that many years later, more than forty years after Tecumseh's visit to the Muskogees in

1811, many false tales had been told about the Great Tucumseh by men who had never seen or heard him. These said he was proud and egotistical. These were false reports. Uriah said that after Truth Teller had returned to the Pitch Tree area, later in 1812, Tecumseh came again . Truth Teller said he went to hear him at Autauga. He followed Tecumseh the next day when he crossed the Coosa and went to Toockabatcha, the ancient capital of the Creeks. Men who were not at this council and had heard only third or fourth-hand reported that Tucumseh and those with him were very pompous and ceremonious. They also said that Tecumseh only pretended to be modest and that he and his Ohio followers had dressed themselves so as to strike terror into the White settlers.

The account, written more than forty years after the event by those who were not there said that Tecumseh and his followers had painted their faces black, had dressed their hair with eagle feathers and had tied white buffalo tails around their waists, letting them trail behind them as they walked and that they adorned their arms in the same fashion. Truth Teller said this description was invented by those who wanted to portray Tecumseh as a false prophet or a pompous fool.

Uriah admitted, somewhat ashamed of the fact, that he had not liked what he had heard his uncle say of the great Tecumseh's brother, the Prophet, who was present at that meeting. He was reputed to be ugly and stupid. When he was a child had been struck in the right eye by an arrow and had also fallen into the fire, burning his face on the left side and thus causing him to bear a disfigured demeanor. Those who disliked and feared him said he had a mean, snarling face. His single eye glared at the whole world, friend and foe alike.

Although Truth Teller did not agree with the great Tecumseh, he admired him, but he too did not like the Prophet, saying he was a liar and a false-hearted man. His prophesies were for his own popularity and were probably false. He had told Uriah that the Prophet had been a drunkard and had used witchcraft before he started on his mission with Tecumseh.

Truth Teller said he had heard that, many years before. The Prophet claimed to have had a vision which told him he was supposed to help lead all his people in this life and in the next. At that time, The Prophet had fallen into a trance and was presumed dead, but as he was about to be buried, he opened his eyes and told those around him that he had seen two beautiful young men who told him the Master of Life was angry with all those in the nation who were given to drunkenness, lying, witchcraft, and stealing, and that unless all the tribes refrained from such wickedness, the Master of Life would destroy them. But, if they refrained from these acts of wickedness as well as other ways of the White man, such as the eating of hogs, of bullocks, and of sheep, they would enter a beautiful place after death. The Great Spirit had given them deer and buffalo for food and they must make their bread of corn and not of wheat. They must not wear linen or woolen apparel, but dress as did their fathers, in skins and furs of animals. He said he had seen the open door of this place, but had not entered. The name he took after this vision was Open Door, Pemsquatawah. He stopped drinking and using most witchcraft and was very severe on those who drank or used any sort of witchcraft different from his own. He was not intelligent and not at all like the great Tecumseh. As long as he followed the directions of Tecumseh, Truth Teller said, The Prophet did little harm, but without Tecumseh he would be dangerous. Truth Teller repeated to Uriah that The Prophet, like himself, had had several names to this point in his life. The name he was best known by before he had visions was Elkswatawa, The Loud Voice, but he changed his name to Pemsquatawah, Open Door, after he became a Prophet and the Whites called him simply The Prophet. He also told Uriah that the Prophet had taken on privileges which belonged to the Chiefs of the tribes. He had, some three years earlier, condemned and put to death several Delaware Chiefs, accusing them of witchcraft. His growing popularity and power alarmed the American governor of the Ohio region, William Henry Harrison, later President of the United States, who warned the tribes against his message, saying,

"My children, this man is a fool. He speaks not the words of the Great Spirit, but the Evil Spirit and of the British agents who are guiding him. Let him cease alarming the White Settlers and go with his followers further north where he can hear the British agents more clearly."

After this rebuke by the Governor, The Prophet and his followers, in 1808, moved to the banks of the Wabash, near the mouth of the Tippecanoe River.

John Pearson listened to Uriah's information and opinions and was of divided mind. On the one hand, he envied his brother such a handsome, graceful son, but on the other hand he was glad he did not have to face the situation in a few years of having to see that son, young as he would still be, choose the way of the Red Sticks and join a fight against the White man which, united or not, they could not win.

They arrived at the school after their two-day ride without incident. Uriah was introduced to the Headmaster and then taken to visit the students. Uriah had thought that he would be the only mixed breed student at the school, but he found that of the 125 or so students, at least one-third had mothers who were Cherokee, Creek or Choctaw and fathers or grandfathers who were French, Irish, Scotch, or English. There seemed to be no distinction made among them. The school master put a full blooded English student in charge of Uriah to show him the school and to explain the schedule and then invited John to remain at the school for a day or two if he liked.

The schoolmaster told John that he had a suggestion to make concerning the treatment of Uriah. "He has reached what we consider the age of reason. He is somewhat older than twelve. He can tell the difference between right and wrong. He is responsible for his actions and his decisions. Instead of automatic expulsion, which we have talked about, I suggest that Uriah, if he commits an action deemed worthy of punishment, be allowed to choose, either expulsion or flogging. If the choice is his, he cannot object if he chooses flogging.'"

John accepted the definition of the age of reason. "What I have seen of my nephew the last few days impresses me. He seems to be a self-possessed, amiable, well-behaved boy. I don't think it likely he will selfishly, or carelessly, transgress any rule which would merit flogging."

"Perhaps not, but as St. Paul has written: 'All have sinned and come short of the glory of God,'" the headmaster replied.

John agreed to put the choice to Uriah, who listened politely while the minister explained his suggestion and again quoted St. Paul.

Uriah was not sure what the White man's word "sin" was, but assumed that if it merited flogging it must be murder, theft, rape or fornication with one's mother or sisters. Since he thought it unlikely that he would ever be guilty of any of these acts, which were also severely punished by the Muskogee, he took a few minutes, weighed the suggestion and agreed to choose, if the time came, but secretly thought that the White man could make no fair rule which he could not, in some fashion obey. The school master invited John to stay and rest after his long ride. He accepted the invitation for one day, but declined a further stay, saying he had urgent business in Charleston and must return there as soon as possible.

"I'm to be married in a month to the loveliest girl in Charleston. I must return to see that all is ready for us to move into our own quarters above the mercantile establishment I've just purchased. I'd like to take care of Uriah's matriculation fees and tell him goodbye before leaving."

This was done and Uriah was to remain at the school for a little over three years, with occasional visits to John and Lucinda in Charleston, whose wedding, all agreed, he could not interrupt his newly-begun studies to attend. These days, he told his granddaughter, were the happiest and most care-free days of his life. He made fast friends there, many of whom became important men in the South, particularly South Carolina, in later years, and learned what the school had to teach of Greek and Latin and English literature. Helping to provide food for the school, he still could hunt and fish and enjoy the forest. Wrestling, running, and competing at stick ball with his companions in the school kept him healthy and provided ample expansion of his sense of self-worth when he won and taught him some humility when he lost. In Charleston he visited the docks as often as possible and received subtle lessons in etiquette from Lucinda, who believed that, even in the wilderness, good manners were to be appreciated, and perhaps there even more than in Charleston.

As his father had predicted, war broke out between the Americans and the English in June 1812, the spring after he entered the school. News was slow in arriving from the Pitch Tree Settlement and from Charleston. He was not to learn until some months after the events the situations which opened the war between the Upper and Lower Creeks in 1811 and the outcome of the battles. Nor was he to learn until he went back to Charleston, where his uncle John had a Boston newspaper several months old that told of the events in the north which had taken place during Tecumseh's journey and mission to the southern tribes.

From the newspaper they learned that The Prophet, during the absence of Tecumseh, in the summer and fall of 1811, had taken on more authority than Tecumseh would have given him, had provoked and dealt in his own name with the White Governor, William Henry Harrison, had fought the White forces and had been defeated .The newspaper gave an account of the battle, called the Battle of Tippecanoe, from the location of The Prophet's village on the banks of the Wabash River, near the mouth of the Tippecanoe River. The newspaper, of course, told the story from the point of view of the army under the direction of William Henry Harrison. The number of warriors on each side was not known, but from the dead, it was conjectured that the forces were about equal. By common consent, the combined forces of the Indians were under the direction of three war chiefs: White Loon, Stone Eater, and Winnemac. The battle was fought contrary to the wishes of Tecumseh, who had not wanted a pitched battle with the Whites until he could form a confederacy of all tribes, north and south. When he, earlier, had told Harrison that all tribes were one people, Harrison was reported to have replied:

"When the White man came to this country, the Miamis were in control of the land of the Wabash and the Shawnees were in the country now called Georgia. The land was purchased from the Miamis. If the Great Spirit had wanted all the tribes to be one people, he would not have given them six different languages."

Hearing this, Tecumseh, in Shawnee fashion, had not replied, but, very angry, had walked away from the conference.

The Boston newspaper article stated that the attack in 1811 on the White soldiers, who had entered the disputed territory in early November 1811, expecting a battle, had been precipitated by General Harrison's having made three demands. He required that all stolen horses should be returned, that Indian murderers of White settlers were to be delivered up to him, and that the Kickapoo, the Pottawatomie, and the Winnebago warriors then at Tippecanoe return to their respective tribes. In a peace parley with The Prophet, both he and The Prophet agreed on another parley before beginning any hostilities. However, as soon as night came, The Prophet had called his warriors together and brought out a magic bowl, a sacred torch, and a string of beads which he told his followers were holy and would, when each touched them, make the warrior invulnerable. If they touched them, the White man's bullets could not harm them. At four o'clock the next morning Harrison, on rising, heard a sentinel's musket shot, and realized that The Prophet had not kept his word and that his warriors were attacking. The newspaper gave a minute account of the actions of the Whites, but told almost nothing of that of the united tribes.

According to the article which John Pearson and Uriah Pearson read, Harrison had lost about 180 men. Indian casualties were not known, but since they had left the dead on the battle field, contrary to their custom, taking away only the wounded, it was assumed that their losses had been considerable.

Little information was given about the combined forces of the tribes, except that during the battle The Prophet had stood on a promontory and recited incantations and war songs, but well out of danger. When the battle went against his forces and he was reproached by his followers for his lies, he told them that his predictions had failed because his wife, unclean as were all women, had touched the sacred bowl and made it unclean also. Deceived and disappointed, his followers deserted and scattered. When Tecumseh, whose Shawnee name was Pounching Big Cat, returned from his journey to the southern tribes, he found both his village and his plans destroyed. Nothing was left of either. The American forces had taken all the corn, beans, and other provisions as well as copper cooking kettles. What they could not carry away they burned and then they burned the entire village.

Tecumseh asked Harrison to arrange a meeting between himself and President Madison. Harrison refused. After Harrison's refusal, Tecumseh, Pouncing Cat, went to join the British in Canada to fight against the Americans in their attempt to annex that country, which they believed should rightly be part of the United States. . He was killed in an early battle, fighting for the British. His corpse was identified only by the fact that he had one leg smaller than the other, causing him to limp slightly and he had a tooth which, though not rotten, was of a slightly blue cast. The British commander rebuked a soldier taking a piece of skin from Tecumseh's leg as a souvenir, and gave the Great Tecumseh a proper burial.

Uriah also learned, but some months after the fact, that his youngest uncle had been killed at the battle of Horseshoe Bend, the first major battle of the Muskogee Red Sticks against the Americans under the Tennessee General Andrew Jackson and his militia and William McIntosh, head of the Lower Creeks of the Coweta Village. Instead of the unity among the tribes, which the great Tecumseh had tried to achieve, civil war between the Creek tribes, dividing the Wind Clan, had now broken out.

The war opened when some mixed breed and full blooded Muskogees, Upper Creeks, went to Florida to purchase guns and ammunition, preparing to retaliate against Georgia and Tennessee irregulars who had stormed a Creek village, killing women and children. They were ambushed as they returned. Mixed breeds led on both sides. No civilians were present and the Upper Creeks won when the Whites began to plunder the pack animals, stealing guns and ammunition, too distracted to continue the fight. The second major skirmish was against a fort, the home of a mixed blooded Creek, Samuel Mims. This too the Upper Creeks won, led by mixed breeds, among whom were William Weatherford, a one-sixteenth Creek called Red Eagle and his cousin, Peter McQueen, a White, Although they won and massacred most of the people in the fort, they lost more than a hundred warriors. A few more skirmishes followed, but with the last battle, the Battle of Horseshoe Bend, the Upper Creeks lost in a decisive battle and with the battle, their Nation.

Chapter IV

War Declared 1812

During his years at the school, Uriah received news from his parents in the Pitch Tree Settlement by way of his Uncle John. His mother and sisters sent letters, money and small things which they had made for him. These were sent to the school along with provisions the schoolmaster had ordered from Charleston. The events there and in Upper Creek territory were relayed only partially to him and the news he did receive was several weeks old. His father had decided that he should not immediately receive news of his young uncle's death. His uncle, three years his senior and considered of age by Muskogee standards, had joined the Red Sticks of his mother's clan, the Wind Clan, whose members were in both the Upper and Lower Creek villages. He was killed in the decisive Battle of Horseshoe Bend.

Daniel Pearson feared his son would leave the school and return to the Pitch Tree Settlement when he was told of the events which had transpired there, but he would then go to join whatever Upper Creek forces were ready to do in retaliation for the massacre. But for the beginning of 1812 he was occupied with his studies, sports, and the occasional much anticipated visit to Charleston to visit John and Lucinda Pearson. John and his father-in-law, McGowan, were preparing for whatever the hostilities might throw them in the way of either profit or loss. Lucinda, preparing for the advent of their first child, was concerned that her husband and father were too interested in profiting by the war and too little concerned with the moral implications of their actions. Both had invested heavily in privateers and both had received initial profits from their investment and anticipated more. Anyone who had a boat, whatever its condition, could outfit as a privateer, since the Federal government, although it had, in the act which declared war, authorized the President to issue letters of marque and reprisal, not yet set standards for commissioning privateers.

In answer to Lucinda's questions and apprehensions as to the morality of an occupation which in peace time would be considered piracy and terrorism, her husband replied, "In the last war, even President Washington owned a one-fourth share of a privateer along with two of his relatives and a fourth party. The late President Jefferson condoned privateers and the *Boston Globe* even published a statement to that effect. This paper is two weeks old, but one of our captains brought it back from Massachusetts. Let me read to you what he said.

"What produces peace? The distress of individuals. What difference to the sufferer is it that his property is taken by a national or private armed vessel? Did our merchants, who have lost 917 vessels by British captures, feel any gratification that most of them were taken by his majesty's men-of-war? Were the spoils less rigidly enforced by a 74-gun ship than by a privateer of four guns, and were not all equally condemned? In the United States every possible encouragement should be given to privateering in time of war with a commercial nation. We have tens of thousands of seamen that without it would be destitute of the means of support, and useless to their country. Our national ships are too few in number to give employment to one-twentieth part of them, or retaliate the acts of the enemy. By licensing private armed vessels, the whole naval force of the nation is truly brought to bear on the foe, and while the contest lasts, that it may have the speedier termination, let every individual contribute his mite, in the best way he can, to distress and harass the enemy, and compel him to peace."

"Yes," replied Lucinda. "I understand that great men can find reasons a plenty to justify their doings. But they stay at home in comfort while the brave or the foolish go to fight the battles they are sent to. What of the families of those killed by the British? How will they survive once their husbands, fathers and brothers are killed pursuing a few dollars while you and my father and others like you profit many times over from an investment that is based on theft and death? I love you, John, and I love my father, but on this we do not agree and never will agree."

Fortunately for John's marital tranquility, Lucinda's preparation for her coming confinement at the birth of their first child prevented the subject from coming up again.

In the first six months of the war, Uriah's uncle and his father-in-law were among the speculators who profited by the fact that most of the naval battles occurred on the open sea by private armed vessels. At the beginning of the war, the Federal government had only about 20 ships. In the next three years American privateers would total more than 500 with all kinds of vessels. These private ships were to capture, burn, or sink and destroy about 1,300 British merchantmen of all classes, while the U. S. Navy captured only about 250. Those sent out from Charleston, along with those from Philadelphia and Portsmouth numbered only about thirty-five. Of these, John Pearson and George McGowan were part owners of two. Such was the damage to British shipping that by 1813, insurance on most British merchant ships was refused and those which were insured were insured for rates at high as 33⅓ percent.

Initial profits for investors at the beginning of the war ran several hundred times more than the original investment, since there were no standards and no regulation by the Federal government. By January of 1814, however, James Monroe, Secretary of State, tried to curtail some of the dangers to the crews and the abuses of the captains by sending to the Collector of Customs in Savannah instructions regarding equipping and arming private vessels, mandating the number of officers and crew, amount of armaments and types of ships. Commissions already issued to ships that did not meet these requirements were to be revoked and new applications by owners of ships of inferior class were to be sent to Washington for review.

While Jonn Pearson and George McGowan were busy making profit on land and on sea, Uriah's father, Daniel Pearson, was still urging neutrality to those in the Pitch Tree area of Georgia. Events there were to prove that his rational and logical arguments, though well received by some, would prove ineffectual against the destruction of Muscogee land and civilization. The powerful chiefs, hoping to gain time, were opposing the war talk of the Red Sticks. In Council they decided that one of the most outspoken of the Red Sticks must be executed as an example to other Red Sticks of both the Upper and Lower Creeks. The warrior chosen for execution was Little Warrior, a major Red Stick. In retaliation for his execution, the Red Sticks in the summer of 1813 attacked the Creek town of Tuckabatchee, on the west side of the Tallapoosa River, beginning a civil war among the Upper and Lower Creeks, an event Daniel Pearson had foreseen and warned against.

This event, as well as the massacre of the White settlers at Fort Mims, called the Whites under Andrew Jackson, General in the Tennessee Militia, into the conflict. The Americans were as ill-organized and as ill-led at the second battle as at the first. Fear of an Indian uprising which was expected to happen in retaliation for the destructions of the Muskogee village of Autossa had led settlers to go to Fort Mims, a makeshift garrison on the lower Alabama River. The commander of the stockade, Major John Beasley, although warned by two slaves that Indians were near, paid no heed and had one slave whipped, although the owner of the second prevented his being whipped, and for this decision opposing the orders of Major Beasley, he was asked to leave the fort the next morning with his family and the slave. Major Beasley maintained that the slaves had invented to story to avoid work and that what they saw were red cows.

The Indians, led by William Weatherford, a one-sixteenth Muskogee, called Red Eagle by the Muskogees and also called Billie Larney by the Whites, with a Muskogee war chief, Menawa, called Crazy War Hunter by the Whites, attacked, shooting arrows wrapped in cloth which they set on fire, and as the out buildings were burning, entered the stockade, slaughtered and scalped all by a few of the fort's inhabitants. The news brought to the Pitch Tree Village, differed from the newspaper account, and from the accounts of those who heard first hand the tales of the actions, both cruel and kind, of those who escaped. Some accounts said that Weatherford, admired both by the Whites and the Indians, had tried to prevent the attack and was not present, having gone several miles away to see after some of the Negroe slaves of his half-brother, Davy Tate, to prevent their being driven away by the Muskogees. Most of the actions reported in the newspapers and by those there were tales of cruelty, but a few reported actions that were kind and brave. After the fort was burned or almost so, all who could not escape, and few did, were slaughtered and scalped. A few, some women and children, were saved by Muskogees or Blacks who knew them and at risk to themselves protected and hid them until the massacre was over and they were able to get out of the burning buildings undetected. One or two men, knowing the Muskogees rarely scalped women, hid until they could undress dead women, dress themselves in their clothes and then place themselves among the dead to avoid discovery and death.

The massacre caused the brawler and semi-literate, Andrew Jackson of the Tennessee Militia, later President of the United States, to enter the conflict. Prior to this time, Jackson had volunteered his services to the Federal government but his offer had been rejected, perhaps because of his reputation. His marriage was initially bigamous, since his wife, when she married Jackson, had thought she was divorced from her first husband, who had not gotten a divorce as he had said he was going to. The wife, Rachel, had taught Jackson to read and write, according to his enemies's stories, but most likely, a woman of some cultivation, she had improved his rudimentary command of educated English.

Jackson had little interest in or compassion for any of the natives in the Carolinas, Alabama, Georgia, or Florida. They were, in his estimate, little better than animals. He did not distinguish between the full-blooded Muskogee and the mixed-breed Muskogee whose father had been Irish, English or Scottish. He had a violent, bitter, prejudiced and unforgiving disposition. He thought he had no superior and was jealous of those who considered themselves his equal. If crossed, he was capable of calling one who differed with him, perhaps one of Indian blood, but better educated, with wider experience and more humane feelings, a "damned long, Indian-looking son-of-a-bitch."

His low opinion of them was strengthened by his greed for their land. He was brought into the war as a result of the Massacre at Fort Mims, the second battle of the Creek Civil War. Jackson himself was a man of touchy pride and when he was called into action by the Tennessee legislature he was recovering from a wound received in a duel caused by an insult to one of his friends.

Little Warrior's assassination had occurred in the late summer of 1813. As soon as Jackson and his Tennessee militia entered the conflict, with the help of William McIntosh and the Lower Creeks, in the fall of the same year, they entered the Upper Creek territory and destroyed two Muskogee towns, Talladega and Tallasahatchee.

Eva's grandfather said that he knew nothing firsthand about William McIntosh, but much by way of both Muskogees and White men. He said McIntosh's father, William McIntosh, Senior was a Scotsman serving as Captain on an English vessel. His father, John McIntosh, had been born in Georgia but had returned to England to claim an inheritance. He had married Senoia Seneha, a Creek of the Wind Clan and reputed to be of great beauty. Their son, William McIntosh, Junior, was followed by another son, Roley, or Roderrick McIntosh, born of a second wife of the Creek Wind Clan, a Cherokee.

The story was told that William McIntosh wanted to send his first son, William, Junior back to England to be educated, but Senoia would not agree and her agreement was necessary under Creek law. William McIntosh, Senior abducted the boy from the Coweta Creek village and put him aboard his ship ready to sail for England. Senoia's brothers, Chief Tuskehenehaw and Chief Tomoc Mico followed and removed the boy forcibly from his father.

After this incident, the son returned to the Coweta Village with his uncles while McIntosh, Senior returned to Savannah to the home of one of his cousins, Barbara McIntosh of Fairhope Plantation. There he married his cousin, Barbara McIntosh. The union produced two children, Barbara McIntosh and William McIntosh, who could not be given the added name of Junior, since William McIntosh of the Coweta Village, the mixed-breed Creek/British, was already known by that name. Thus, William McIntosh, who became Chief of Coweta Village had a half-brother who was half Muskogee and half White, Roly McIntosh, and a half-brother and half-sister who were full Whites. He spent some of his childhood in Savannah with his father and stepmother and received the rudiments of an education. He met there his Troup cousins who were McIntoshes through their mother. One of these cousins, George Troup, later became Governor of Georgia. Another Governor, David Mitchell, was the father-in-law of one of McIntosh's daughters.

As an adult, William McIntosh, Junior, also called by his Creek relatives, Tustunnuggee, White Warrior, married three wives: Susanna Coe, a half Creek, Peggy, a Cherokee, and Elizabeth Grier. Each wife lived in her own house with her children on one of his three plantations.

And then, early in the following spring, on March 27, 1814, with 3,000 men, Jackson attacked at Horseshoe Bend, a bend in the Tallapossa River, the Red Stick Warriors of the Upper Creeks who, with some Lower Creek volunteers had decided to make a stand, but were unprepared and still had women and children behind a barricade. The Tennessee forces killed more than 800 Muskogees, both warriors and women and children. Davy Crockett, who participated in the slaughter, later a member of the Texan forces at the Battle of the Alamo, reported, "We shot them all like dogs."

With this battle the Creeks lost their nation and their land. The conquered territory would go to Jackson and to other White land speculators. After the Battle of Horseshoe Bend, Jackson, called by the Indians Jacksa Chula Harjo, made it clear that he wanted land to compensate him and the Tennessee legislature for the cost to them of the war.

Jackson forced the Creeks to sign a treaty giving up 25,000,000 acres, half of Alabama and part of southern Georgia, to the Whites. This land would go to Jackson and to other White land speculators. The Upper Creeks were left with a small strip of land near the Tallapoosa River.

The Lower Creek territory in northern Georgia remained, for the moment, intact. William McIntosh, Chief of Coweta Village and of the Lower Creeks, received a commission as a

Major General in the United States Army and retained private land in northern Georgia. His major plantation, Indian Springs, some few miles south-east of the Pitch Tree Settlement was the major home of two of his three wives, one Creek, one Cherokee, and their families. The third wife, Elizabeth Grieson lived on an adjacent plantation.

Uriah's uncle, hardly older than he, had joined the Upper Creek Red Sticks just prior to the battle of Horseshoe Bend. By Muskogee law he was of age and able to make his own decisions and judgments. He was shot and killed early in the battle. After Jackson's militia and their Lower Creek allies had finished the slaughter, McIntosh's Lower Creeks were taking scalps and piling the dead bodies in stacks for burning.

One, seeing Uriah's dead uncle, hacked off his head and threw it to another. "Here, take this scalp. That's the one who defeated you in the spring games last year. Now his people will see who's the better man."

The other dropped it on the ground. "I don't need his scalp to prove who's the better man. This battle proves we're all better men."

An Upper Creek friend who had survived by hiding behind several dead logs and witnessed the scene, waited until the Lower Creeks had started the fire and had then left to clean the scalps. He hastily left his hiding place and retrieved the severed head. Later, after nightfall, he found a canoe still intact which Jackson's men had not set adrift or burned, and hiding in the bottom, set it free from its moorings and drifted downstream until he thought he was safe and out of danger.

He took the head to an encampment of women, children, and old men who had escaped the slaughter. There the women preserved the head in brine. This he took back to Sapehunka, his sister, and Truth Teller, his brother. Uriah's mother kept the head of her brother preserved in her house and the story of the massacre in her heart against the day of reckoning.

Truth Teller, Daniel Pearson, and John Pearson decided that the story of his uncle's participation in the battle and his death should be kept as long as possible from Uriah, for fear that he would attempt to join the few remaining Upper Creeks who were still fighting skirmishes against Jackson's outposts, all of which they lost. Although news of the defeat reached the school in the late Spring, Uriah did not hear the details concerning his uncle until his summer holiday visit to Charleston. Told the news, Uriah accepted the facts, questioned only the delay in his learning of his uncle's death. His anger was quiet and deep. Just as his mother, he kept his anger in his heart until he could take revenge for his uncle's death and the loss of the land of the Wind Clan in Upper Creek territory.

After hearing the news of his Uncle's death, Uriah, thought a long time before deciding to go to his Uncle John with his decisions. "My father was right in many of the things he said. The Muskogees of the Upper Creeks have lost all by joining the British against the Americans, but he was wrong in telling my mother that I wouldn't learn at the White man's school. I have worked hard and have learned those things that he thinks important for a White man. I speak English well now. I'm told so by the schoolmaster. I've also mastered whatever I've been given in Latin and Greek. In fact, the schoolmaster has had me help the entering students in those languages. He has offered to pay me to continue doing that when I return to the school. I've decided not to return. It's time I establish myself somewhere so I can put to profit what I've learned and be of use to my people. If you'll help me, I'm going to find a privateer and ship out with it on its next trip. Before that, I'll go back to the Pitch Tree Settlement to see my family and tell them what I've decided. I am, as you know, older than the age that the Muskogees consider to be a man."

Neither Truth Teller nor John Pearson was surprised at his decision, but neither agreed with it. Although the privateers were more often than not successful at the beginning of the war, death, as well as terrible injuries, were frequent. The United States government had voted to pay pensions to those fighting on privateer vessels if they were wounded or disabled, but no one had very much faith in that government, and those disabled were frequently made a burden to their families and friends. Uriah, with no sea experience, indeed very little experience of any kind, was likely to be one of those wounded or disabled. Each advised delay before a decision was made and Uriah, still firm in his decision, left to return briefly to the Pitch Tree Settlement, a journey he would repeat several times during his lifetime. The last time he went he would avenge himself on the Tennessean of his youth as well as on McIntosh and the other traitor Muskogees who signed the Treaty of Indian Springs with the Americans, giving up all remaining Muskogee lands in Georgia and Alabama, excluding that of McIntosh.

Chapter V

The Interim

Eva's grandfather lived to be a very old man. After the Indian Wars and after the War of Secession, he said that when he was a young man, before his mind began to turn backward and to judge the events of his past life, that he had thought himself always in control of his decisions and of his actions. He said he had not realized that both he and those around him, both Whites and Muskogees, were like fallen tree branches which, landed in a swift and powerful river, swirled along in the current of that river, never to control where nature and fate carried them. When he returned to the Pitch Tree Settlement, he was between 15 and 16 years old, having spent a little more than three years in Charleston and in the school north of Charleston. He thought his obligations and his desires coincided. He must, he thought, make his own way, and the fastest way seemed to lead to sailing with the privateers, sharing with the crew his small part of the booty captured. Having lived three or more years as a White man he now decided to continue in the White world and to gain experience as a sailor among White men his equals.

He saw, when he returned to his village, that little of everyday life had changed, but he was surprised that his father was not so tall as he had remembered him and that there were traces of grey in the hair above his ears. His mother he contrasted with the White women he had seen in Charleston and particularly with his Uncle John's wife, Lucinda, who had a pale complexion, and who had hair the color of light honey which curled about her face before being held in pins on top of her head or behind her neck. Her eyes were blue-grey, changing color with whatever she wore. She was slight in build, being about five feet four with small bones. His mother, he noticed for the first time, was beautiful, but entirely different from Lucinda. Her skin was the color of the planed and aged walnut trees and her straight hair was very dark but not coarse and, when not pulled back from her forehead into a severe knot behind her neck, or plaited into one or two braids, was so long that she could sit on it. Her eyes were dark brown, inclining to black. She was taller than Lucinda, about five feet seven or eight. Her bones small, but her back was very stiff and straight. He did not recognize his two sisters, who had been seven and nine when he left and were now matured almost into young womanhood. They were shy, not recognizing him either. The family had increased by the birth of a baby boy.

After greetings and information had been exchanged, he was first taken to the Council house where he was reintroduced to Council Members by his uncle, Hoponika Futsakia, The Truth Teller. He answered their questions as fully as he could, suddenly recognizing that he had not spoken his first language for several years and that he lacked words from time to time. That realization startled and disturbed him, because in his own mind he was still a Muskogee and was only experimenting with being a White, no matter what his recent education. Later he was to visit with his mother, who showed him the pickled head of his uncle, killed at the Battle of Horseshoe Bend. Much decomposed, the head was still recognizable. She told him that she had kept it so that she could show it to him and that she would now bury it. He and Truth Teller, her oldest brother, were adult Wind Clan members responsible for avenging his death when the time came. All clans except the Wind Clan had limits on the time during which murders could be avenged. There was no limit on the Wind Clan. The recently born son would have other Wind Clan obligations, since he was too young for this.

If the battle between the Muskogee and the Whites continued, as his father said it would, then at that time the last child might be old enough to fight. His father said that, although the Muskogees of upper Georgia, the Cherokees and the Lower Creeks, kept their land for the present, that fact would change when the Whites from Tennessee and the Carolinas, who continued to encroach on Muskogee territory, pushed even further into Georgia and Alabama.

Uriah spent somewhat more than a month among his Muskogee people and found life there so pleasant that he almost lost his desire to try his fate on the sea, but he understood that if he ever lived as a White man, and his father assured him that he might sometime have to, he would need money. He left regretfully and returned to Charleston to his uncle and aunt's house. Changes had been occurring there also, but since he had lived among his White Charleston relatives for several years, they had been so gradual he was not as aware of them. John's father-in-law, George McGowan, had achieved his dual ambition, to enter Charleston society and to build a plantation house on his 5,000 acres. The first he had managed by marrying the widow of a Charleston aristocrat, the second by way of the fortune he had accumulated from his investment in two privateers and from the fact that his inventory had lasted from 1811 through 1813. His Irish son-in-law ironically suggested that the two facts were related more closely than McGowan would admit. John Pearson himself had benefited more than he could have foreseen. With his newly acquired fortune he told Lucinda that after he had repaid the merchant Rouglin, he intended to buy land on the end of the peninsula, near his warehouses, and build a five-story house with a carriage house, a separate house for her house slaves, and a garden at the rear. Lucinda found both her father's project and that of her husband pretentious. However, she was overruled by John and, later, as her family increased, numbering finally eight, counting her husband and herself, she admitted that he had been right in his foresight.

But for the moment, the only future Uriah was concerned with was that of his naval career. Neither his father, Truth Teller, nor John Pearson agreed with his decision to sail as an apprentice on a privateer, but they all decided that, since he could not be dissuaded, and was of age by Muskogee standards, the best thing to do was to choose a ship which was to sail in the waters close to the United States coast line. To this point in the war England had been too busy fighting Napolean and his conquered territories to have sufficient men and ships to do little but blockade New England and Canadian ports. The few warships available to protect merchant ships the British could spare for southern waters made sailing there less risky and more profitable. They thus placed him on a ship whose captain both Uriah and his uncle had known for some time and of which John Pearson and George McGowan owned, together, half interest.

They sailed out of Charleston at the end of the year, bound for Jamaica to pick up a cargo, primarily of rum. Unexpectedly, a short distance from Jamaica, they spotted a British merchant ship of about the same size and number of armaments. The captain cleared the deck for action, closing all exits from the decks to the holds below, a practical method of being sure that no one could avoid the coming action.

His own ship, much lighter and faster than the British merchantman, he maneuvered so as to ram its stern. Shouting, screaming men and boys jumped and climbed onto the enemy

British ship. Slashing, stabbing, dodging enemy swords and knives, the experienced sailors as well as the newly recruited boys fought hand to hand, the entire action lasting for almost an hour. Almost 250 men crowded on the ship's deck. Uriah said that he did not know whether or not he had killed any of the men he stabbed or slashed because the action was so fast and so confused that sometimes more than one person attacked the same enemy, but he thought it quite likely that in the chaos his blows had killed at least some or hastened their end if they had previously been struck by someone else. After the action subsided, the only persons left alive among the British were about 50 wounded and the ship's doctor. The dead among the enemy were thrown overboard, but the wounded were taken below to be tended by the doctor.

The Americans had lost only one dead and five wounded. The dead sailor and the five wounded were put back on the American privateer to return to Charleston with the booty. An examination of the ship and its contents found that in addition to the British ship, which was a valuable prize, the cargo was comprised of silver originally from Mexican mines to be taken to England and worked into sterling flatware, vases, platters and decorative objects and sent back again to wealthy South American families.

A smaller amount of the cargo consisted of rich household furnishings being returned to England for use by those returning to their homeland: Chinese rugs, wall hanging, and bolts of silk. The total value of the cargo, not counting the value of the ship, was estimated at upwards of $100,000.

Uriah's share, even though small, made him think himself comparatively rich, since he had never had any money except that sent to him via his uncle to be used for someone to do his laundry and a small amount of money to spend when he visited Charleston.

The ship did not complete its voyage to Jamaica, but docked

at Savannah with its prize and cargo. The members of the crew were paid there and were free to find another ship on which to sign on if they chose.

Uriah said that while visiting Savannah he had had time to review his sea-going adventure and to analyze his life and his choices. He liked the companionship of his shipmates, the sea air, the feeling of freedom while on the sea. However, he remembered, more than he wanted to, the fight, which produced blood on the deck deep enough and wide spread enough to cause all the fighters to slip and slide, and he remembered too the screams of the dying and the wounded. To have to do such slaughter, he thought, there must be a deep duty toward family or a need to protect oneself. Neither applied to the battle he had participated in. He thought of Truth Teller and what he would say. He knew that his uncle would tell him that he had behaved like a White man who fought for money, and not like a member of the Wind Clan, who fought only to protect themselves or their families and land.

But, because he wanted to continue in the way he had recently chosen, Uriah reminded himself that he was half White and free to choose the way of the White man as many mixed breeds had before him. But, since he was honest with himself he remembered that he had explained to his uncle John the way of the Muskogee which he had said his White father did not understand. Now, if he chose the way of the White man, he would have to violate many of the ways of the Muskogee.

Still, Truth Teller would also have reminded him that as a Muskogee his enemies were not the British but the Tennessee Americans and the half-breeds of the Lower Creeks. They had invaded his land, killing not only Red Stick warriors, but women and children and they had burned their villages and crops. He rationalized that the fact that the British would also have done the same thing in the same circumstances did not apply, since they had not. Nevertheless, he put these reservations at the back of his mind, telling himself that he would decide later if he was a White man or a Muskogee after he had tasted a little more the life of a White man and he agreed to ship out again in a few weeks on a larger ship for a longer voyage.

Savannah he found even more interesting than Charleston. The harbor was just as busy and the goods to be shipped if the blockade could be run were not indigo and rice but cotton. Charleston seemed larger but the city of Savannah was laid out in a more logical fashion. The founders had interspersed green areas with beautiful trees and plants every several blocks, giving the whole an atmosphere of one big garden. The houses were equally impressive and beautiful. His only regret was that he could not and would not be invited to visit the interiors. From open doorways when servants were cleaning doors, windows or porches he glimpsed elegant and luxurious interiors representing a life he could have no part of.

While in Savannah he contacted the Jewish immigrant Rouglin, who was now living with the daughter formerly in Charleston and her family, entrusting him with his share of the booty and asking him to convey it to his uncle John at the earliest opportunity. John had accumulated enough money from his privateering investments to repay the balance remaining on the loan made to him by Rouglin when he purchased Rouglin's property on the wharves in Charleston.

Uriah had a double reason for visiting the merchant Rouglin. When he had left the school the schoolmaster had not only offered him a position as an assistant where he could continue his reading and his education, but had suggested that, if he would not stay, perhaps he would return to Charleston and find some reputable lawyer who would let him read for the law with him. After a few years, if he found the law interesting, he might set himself up as a lawyer. Uriah had not totally rejected the idea, but thought that if he decided to do so, Savannah would be just as good a city to settle in as Charleston and that he would be more independent in Savannah than in Charleston.

Uriah's decision to ship out again aboard a privateer disturbed both his father and John Pearson. Up until mid 1813, the danger in southern waters had been considerably less than in those near New England and Canada. England in the first year and a half of the war had been too occupied fighting Napoleon and his allies and the necessary reestablishment of a friendly government, both in France and in the countries of Napoleon's former conquests and allies. After Napoleon's defeat at Waterloo, they were free to give their attention to what they considered a minor skirmish. All battles attempting to annex Canada had failed. In the land battles the English had been successful or had halted the American attacks in major areas of Canada. Some months after the Battle of Horseshoe Bend, not only had the Americans not been successful, but the British had managed to invade the territorial United States. Arriving in Washington D.C., they had, on August 24–25, 1814, routed the defenders there and caused President Madison and his wife to flee into the countryside. The dinner ready and placed on the dining table for the President and Mrs. Madison, was eaten by British officers, who then burned the White House. The British were then in a position to begin sending both warships and English privateers to all ports of the United States by the end of 1813, following the defeat of Napoleon in 1812.

Even so, at the beginning of 1814 the United States was in a position to begin adding frigates to its navy. In July of that year, a two-decker was launched at Charleston and the keels for two others were laid out, but were not completed until after the war was over. In spite of the fact that these ships could be and needed to be built, the United States by the fall of 1814 was insolvent. However, the American privateers, the "sea devils" the British merchants were so afraid of, were still usually successful when they could engage the enemy on the open seas, but the British blockade became tighter around the southern seaboard, and in fact British warships as well as British privateers infested the waters off Charleston and Savannah and fewer ships were able to make a successful run into the open Atlantic and fewer still were interested in attempting it.

The ship Uriah found which would take him on as an apprentice seaman was bound for a longer voyage than the first he had sailed on and for a longer voyage than he really wanted.

The privateer was out of New York but had put into Savannah to pick up supplies and to find replacements for several sick crew members. So, trusting that his decision was the correct one, Uriah signed on in March.

The first part of the voyage was pleasant, he said, and without incident, though full of back-breaking toil for one not used to manual labor. The ship cruised off the Florida coast and at the end of April they sighted three ships under the protection of a large English brig. The merchantmen were English, Russian, and Spanish. At the sight of the privateer, the three small merchant ships fled. Uriah's captain made for the armed English brig and a major battle commenced. At the very beginning of the battle, Uriah's captain commanded a close encounter with the enemy ship and the British brig hit the rigging of the American ship by a broadside, making the American privateer unable to maneuver so that the contest depended on the expertise of the gunners.

At the end of half an hour the enemy ship was extensively damaged and had lost 25 men dead or disabled. The American privateer had lost no one and had only two men wounded. The British ship struck her colors and the Americans boarded to take possession of their prize. The American officers estimated that the vessel would sell for at least 60,000 dollars. On board was 120,000 dollars in specie. Since the southern coast of the United States was now teeming with British warships, the captain decided that it would be prudent to send the captured British ship back to Savannah rather than risk her being recaptured by the British.

Uriah recounted with amusement:

"That decision luckily ended my second cruise and my naval career in a strange way, but safely, and was one of the shortest privateer sorties on record, I'm sure. With several other inexperienced seamen, I was put on board the captured prize. We were fewer than twenty in all, and we started to make out way back to Savannah. But off the coast of Florida, we sighted two British frigates. The American ship we had been on, the privateer, ran to the southward while we, in the prize, continued toward Savannah. The privateer outran one of the British frigates, but we were so clumsy as seamen that we moved too slowly and the second British frigate lowered two boats full of armed men to chase, board and retake our prize. They were gaining on us when the First Lieutenant in charge of our captured prize with all of us 16 frightened, inexperienced boys used the trumpet to order us to prepare to fire a broadside at the approaching boats. As if we could have done that! But, not knowing that our vessel had fewer than 20 men and would have been incapable of defending the ship, the men in the enemy boat, hearing the order, fled, leaving us to return in safety to Savannah."

Uriah said that his two voyages satisfied his desire for an active life on the sea and he returned to Savannah to council with the merchant Rouglin. The merchant told Uriah that his best chance for success in securing a position with a reputable lawyer would be to return to Charleston where his uncle and his uncle's father-in-law were known and had connections to both reputable businessmen and to at least some of Charleston's semi-closed society. If he chose to remain in Savannah, he would help him find a lawyer there, but as a Jew, much of

Savannah's social and professional life were as closed to him as it would be to a mixed-breed Muskogee.

"I'm old and I have my daughters' families. We have few social contacts in Savannah except with the few Jews who are here. Charleston, of course, has more Jews than any city in the South. But we do not suffer from isolation here. We have never been active socially and are most often busy with our businesses or with our families. But you are young and will need both an active social life and a busy intellectual life for the next four or five years if you expect to succeed as an attorney among the Whites. Think over my suggestions and let me know what you decide. I'll help anyway I can. If you'd like me to place your privateering earnings here in Savannah, I think I can do so with a considerable profit to you, but your uncle and father-in-law can do the same in Charleston."

Uriah told his granddaughter that, although he recognized and admitted the reality of the situation as Rouglin stated it, his ego was wounded to acknowledge that his mixed-breed status would be a hindrance to his ambitions in a city where his origins were not known. He told her that he had become so accustomed to being treated as an equal by his uncle and his family as well as by Lucinda's father and the men he had sailed with on his two voyages that he half thought that he could pass for a full-blooded White because he looked very much like some of the French/Spanish he had met as well as like his Irish father. But aside from the prejudice which he probably would encounter in Savannah, his longing to see his family again and to settle into a way of life he was familiar with made him choose to return to Charleston.

The return overland trip to Charleston, although Savannah and Charleston were only about 100 miles apart as the crow flies, took longer than the journey from the Pitch Tree Settlement to the same destination. Travel was through the Low Country, which had less variation of topography than the descent from the mountains of northern Georgia to Charleston on the Atlantic. The merchant Rouglin had arranged for him to join a trading group, and for the trip he had changed into Muskogee clothing and became again a non-White. The trading party was comprised of Whites, Creeks, Seminoles and Blacks, some full-blooded, some of mixed blood. Uriah said that, dressed as a Muskogee, he joined the Muskogee and Black section of the party.

Once past the Savannah River, the trading group had to skirt the low marshy land which had almost no variation until they had climbed onto higher ground some 20 miles inland, making the distance more than 100 miles. The Indians called the area of the Savannah River, Sowanokee Hatchee Thlocka, meaning Big River of the Glades. There was also little variation in the few settlements which they crossed until they were near Charleston.

The Indians they met lived much as did the Whites. There were no villages inhabited solely by Muskogees. The Indians in eastern Georgia and the Carolinas had lived in close proximity with the White man for more than a century. Many, indeed most, were of mixed blood and heritage and found the ways of the White man to their liking. This was one of the primary reason they had joined William McIntosh, a mixed-breed, and those of the Coweta Village against the Upper Creeks, who had resisted assimilation by the Whites, and the Seminoles, who were to resist assimilation even longer, well into the 20th century.

Once back in Charleston, Uriah sought the help of his uncle and of George McGowan, his uncle's father-in-law. Finding a reputable lawyer to let him read law with him and to serve as his assistant was easier than he had anticipated, thanks to the help of McGowan's new wife. As his uncle John had ironically suggested, economics as much as affection had brought about McGowan's marriage to a member of the older aristocracy of Charleston. His wife, Lise, was the widow of an English planter. She herself was the only child of a Huguenot family which had immigrated to Charleston in the preceding century. Her husband followed the English aristocracy's custom of entailing property to the oldest male relative. She did not, on his death, receive any of his real property, which went to their only child, a son, although he did provide in his will that she should receive both his furniture and that which she had brought with her on their marriage. Their only son and his wife inherited the town house and the plantation. Since McGowan, still a robust man and in his 50's, had just completed his plantation house, his proposal was accepted as being to the advantage of both. His new wife, Lise, had fallen out with her son because of her relationship with her daughter-in-law. The estrangement occurred over the ownership of a sterling flatware set, which she said belonged to her Huguenot family, but which her daughter-in-law also claimed as belonging to her family, and which her daughter-in-law kept, saying possession was nine-tenths of the law. As a result, in retaliation, Lise had made a will leaving all her household possessions to John Pearson's wife, Lucinda. Much to her amusement, Lucinda would, with that inheritance, then became a member of the aristocracy, since the distinction between the aristocracy and the "new money" had recently been redefined.

At the end of the War of 1812 many of the merchants, most not members of the aristocracy, had become enormously wealthy. These were cynically termed, by the older aristocracy of Charleston, as "people who bought their own furniture." The aristocracy, of course, had inherited theirs. Lucinda, upon inheriting her stepmother's possessions would, by the new definition, become a member of Charleston's aristocracy.

The prospect amused Lucinda and delighted John, who, although he pretended he did not, as did his father-in-law, George McGowan, set store by class divisions in Charleston, he was secretly as desirous as his father-in-law to enter the class he pretended to ignore or disdain.

Uriah said he once heard John and his wife discussing their different points of view on slavery and on privateering.

"I treat my slaves extremely well," Lucinda argued. "You've refused to admit you also own them, although you do, legally. They're better off here in Charleston where I can feed them, take care of them when they're sick and see that their children are not sold as field hands or worse. Or, if they must be sold, I can see at least that they are placed in honorable houses where they'll not be abused. With me they will receive at least the rudiments of an education. The girls are taught fine needlework and how to cook and serve a well-prepared and elegant meal. This learning will serve them well if they have to leave us and enter another household. They'll be household servants there and not treated roughly or re-sold, since they have valuable skills. They might not learn these things when they are young and in another house."

To this defensive explanation, he heard John reply,

"My dear, you'll never understand that there are some, of whatever color or in whatever land, who would appreciate and enjoy this relatively easy life and comfort at the expense of their freedom, but that there are others who would trade all of this comfort and safety for the right to choose their own way, to make their own decisions, even if these led to failure and death, so long as the choices were made in the free air. As far as privateering is concerned, our country had no navy. Without privateers we would have been easily occupied by the British. And, in addition, the British also have privateers who would have robbed us if they could. Our captains were better fighters and better seamen in better and lighter ships. I have no apology to make for the profit I made in helping our country defeat the British on the sea."

With a light kiss he reminded his wife that they had agreed

on their wedding day never to end a day with a quarrel. Lucinda laughed and agreed. "All right, I'll agree to be a member of Charleston society, even if entry will come by way of a set of British sterling flatware which my stepmother couldn't bring with her to my father's plantation. Since I've inherited my mother's furniture, and will inherit Lise's, I'll be a legitimate member of Charleston society by the new definition. However, there is one thing I refuse to accept, as you refuse to accept my slaves. I'll not accept ownership of the British sterling pieces, or the crystal and china which you received as partial payment for your privateering investment in captured British vessels. These will, in spite of what the law says, always belong to you alone."

With a good-humored smile and shrug, John replied, "Well, who knows? Maybe our children will adopt both our opinions as they will inherit both out possessions. The one thing I'm sure we can agree on is that we have beautiful children."

And so the day ended in peace on both sides.

The marriage of John Pearson's father to a Charleston aristocrat, Uriah said, facilitated his finding someone reputable to read law with. He said the next five years were like a prolonged adolescence. During the day he read law and worked as a clerk in the law office. In the evenings, as Lucinda's nephew-in-law, and thereby acquainted with her stepmother's friends, he enjoyed all Charleston had to offer of pleasant society. In the winter all those who could do so moved to the plantations to oversee the next year's planting, to make repairs, and to visit with neighbors. In the summer everyone moved back to the city to get away from the stifling heat and humidity of the low-lying plantation rice fields and to enjoy the sea breezes of Charleston. Uriah said he flirted with and courted most of the eligible maidens of Charleston society and then moved on to flirt with and court some of their mothers. Many of the husbands found his flirtation and courtship of their wife a glad relief from the complaints of their wife in the long winter days and the long summer nights. Others were less accommodating, and Uriah said he barely escaped serious repercussions once or twice with husbands who were jealous of their wives flirtations.

During this time John Pearson's family grew, Lucinda having a new child every two years. John's five-story city main house was completed, although he kept adding slave quarters; the slaves inhabiting them, he said, belonged to Lucinda, since in theory he did not believe in slavery. His Jesuitical distinction both exasperated and amused Lucinda. The war over, evidence of wealth was everywhere in Charleston. The war itself had ended shortly after Uriah returned to Charleston but had ended with neither side proving or winning anything. The former colonists had not managed to take Canada and join it to increase the number of the current states and the British had not succeeded in retaking even a part of the former colonies.

There was a different story in the Indian Territories. The civil war begun in 1811 still pitted Upper Creeks against Lower Creeks, Choctaws and Cherokees. The latter tribes, since they had fought with the Americans, primarily the Tennesseeans, had not yet lost territory but there was distrust among all the tribes. General Jackson and, by now, William McIntosh, who had been made a general, as head of the Lower Creeks, had advanced into Seminole country in Florida and were pursuing the war there.

Chapter VI

Alabama/Georgia 1822–1824

After defeating the Upper Creeks and forcing them to sign a treaty giving over the major portion of their land to the United States, Jackson and his friends lost no time in dividing up the Territory. The Battle of New Orleans, over in 1815, place names were given to sections of former Upper Creek territory by 1816. Montgomery, Alabama, had a settler as early as 1816 and Selma, Alabama, followed with two more settlers, cousins, in 1817. Shortly thereafter, a former general in the Tennessee militia put up a steam mill near the Selma settlement. Other sections at first kept the place names given by the Muskogee, although as the country brought in more Whites from the Carolinas and Georgia, these were frequently changed. Bibb County, so named in 1820, had begun as Catawba County, keeping the Muskogee name for the area.

Whites and Muskogees formerly occupying the land in villages were officially dispossessed but continued to co-exist with the newly arrived settlers who had divided the land into legal units.

A very small section of land was reserved for the Muskogees, too small for the remnants of those surviving Jackson's almost annihilation of the Upper Creek Muskogees and their Red

Stick allies at the Battle of Horseshoe Bend. Those who did not approve of Chief, and now General, McIntosh's handling of the Lower Creek territory had moved to Upper Creek Territory where there were land speculators and where the army had established forts and tried to keep the peace. The Muskogees had no legal rights there, but they were tolerated for the time being. Their co-existence was not, ultimately, without conflict, both legal and physical.

Uriah said that he heard much from the newly ceded territory where some of the Wind Clan still had a tenuous hold. He decided that, since he had finished his apprenticeship in the law office, and since at least two of the Charleston husbands seemed ready to change their irritation at his relationship with their wives into action, he would be well advised to change his lifestyle and Upper Creek Territory seemed a good choice.

Prior to trying a new beginning in the area he had chosen, Talladega, near where his uncle had been killed in the Battle of Horseshoe Bend, he made another visit to his family in Lower Creek Territory at the Pitch Tree Settlement near Coweta Village, strong hold of General McIntosh, chief of the village and principal land owner. At the end of the War with Britain in 1815, Muskogees, both Creeks and Cherokees who had fought with and for General Jackson were rewarded. Chiefs, scouts, and interpreters were given land, titles and money. McIntosh was made a Major General and added to his wealth with additional land, finally having four plantations and three wives as well as sufficient money to stock the plantations with cattle and horses.

When Uriah reached his parents at their trading post he found many things changed. There were more White settlements on Muskogee land. Both Cherokees and Whites were fencing off portions of Muskogee territory and planting crops, although in theory the Muskogee Creeks of the Lower Creek Confederacy still had control and had not ceded their land as had the Upper Creeks. Lower Creek Chiefs who had not supported General Jackson and who had opposed William McIntosh were trying to maintain sovereignty over land which the Federal government by treaty had agreed would not be open to White settlement.

In an effort to avoid the fate of the Upper Creeks and lose in open confrontation with General Jackson and the Whites, these chiefs had begun as early as 1811, but continuing into 1820, to try two ways to avoid annihilation. First, they decreed that no one could sell any further land without unanimous consent of all of the Chiefs of all Muskogees villages, and second, they began developing a written code of long established customs in order to avoid misunderstandings with the settlers and the Georgia officials. Several versions of the latter were drafted and the final code was published in 1824. These two attempts helped, in part, to maintain relative peace in the Lower Creek towns for a short time.

When Uriah reached the Pitch Tree Settlement he found his father more pessimistic than usual. He told Uriah, "This situation will not hold. The South Carolina and Tennessee farmers and trappers coming into Creek territory are like waves coming to shore at full tide. The first waves are small but they will be followed by bigger and stronger waves. Anyone standing in the way will be engulfed and swept off his feet. I think our family is safe here for a few more years. But I also think it would be wise to pay a visit to what remains of the Upper Creek clan in Alabama as well as to investigate how the Whites are selling and settling the former Creek land there. If the situation here becomes violent, as it well may in a few years, we may have to settle as Whites in the area near Talladega, where, I'm told, Whites and Muskogees seem to coexist peacefully, at least for the moment."

He also told Uriah that the Red Stick warrior who had escaped the Horseshoe Bend Massacre by General Jackson had returned to the area and had learned that the few survivors had taken what remained of the old men, the women and children to relative safety.

After the almost annihilation at Horseshoe Bend, some chiefs attempted to save what few remained of their villages. Some sent their women and children into hiding near the head waters of the Catoma River, placing warriors to protect them in the cane brakes nearby; others placed them on a little island in the Alabama River; still others took their people near the falls of Cahawba, where they were able to remain for more than a year after Jackson forced the signing of a peace treaty dispossessing all the Upper Creeks.

But when Jackson built his fort, which he called Fort Jackson and moved his troops there, most of the chiefs became discouraged and admitted defeat. Some few, such as William Weatherford, called Red Eagle, a cousin of General McIntosh, and Igillis Ineha, called Menauway, were pardoned, but most were shot or hanged. The most reckless, as well as the bravest and some of the last to surrender, Josiah Francis, called the Prophet, and Nehe Marthla Micco, the Otisee chief, were hanged in 1818, four years after the defeat at Horseshoe Bend.

Sapehunka recounted these things to Uriah and reminded him that his uncle's death at Horseshoe Bend had not yet been avenged. Although it was not always the White man's way, she said her husband, Daniel Pearson understood the way of the Muskogee. The Wind Clan would avenge his young uncle's death in time, but she still cautioned him that the time for revenge was not yet. Uriah reflected that while he was privateering and remaining safe and relatively at his ease in a law office in Charleston, his Muskogee brothers were fighting for their lives and for their way of life. Even if he was a Lower Creek Muskogee and their territory still relatively intact, his Wind Clan had no divided loyalties. He was part of both Upper and Lower Creek villages and many, like his youngest uncle, who, even though a member of the Lower Creeks, had fought with the Upper Creek Red Sticks. He discussed with his father his plans to visit Talladega. He said it was one of the few times he and his father were in agreement.

"Your decision is a good one," his father said. "For many years your mother's Wind Clan ties have protected both me and her children. Now it may soon be time that my skin color and language will have to be used to protect us all. The men coming from Tennessee and South Carolina are in many ways less civilized than any of what the Whites call the Five Civilized Tribes. No Muskogee will be safe in this territory in a few years. The first White men to come will be those who leave behind the least but have the most to gain here. The violence will consume all of the Muskogee land left. I don't want to expose your mother and sisters to that situation. You brother will still be too young to help protect them. The thieves and liars among the Whites will outnumber the honest farmers when they first begin to settle here. The Muskogee who does not lie will be at the mercy of those among the White men who cheat, lie and steal. You may now understand why I insisted that you be educated as a White man. As a Muskogee, you will, I hope, retain the integrity of your mother's people but have the ability to function as a decent White man as a result of your education.

"I'm told by Muskogees who pass through here from the Upper Creek villages that, although the villages have been burned and almost destroyed, some few individual houses have remained and the Creeks there have cooperated with the honest farmers who are moving into their former villages and hunting grounds. The land is being laid off in sections and can be bought from land speculators. One of the major speculators is General Jackson. I think it would be wise for you to go to the area around Talladega and see what is happening there and check to see if this report is correct. We may have to move the trading post there. I think I can now trust your judgment.

My only request is that if you decide to buy land in that vicinity, you do not buy land from anyone representing General Jackson. I'm told by the Whites that, while some call him 'Old Hickory,' a great many others call him 'Old Slickery.'"

Flattered that he had at last achieved a favorable review from his father, Uriah cut short his planned visit and started the following day for the Upper Creek territory. When he had crossed the river separating Upper and Lower Creek Villages, the landscaped changed.

Even though the last major battle had ended with the defeat of the Upper Creeks in 1814, eight years later the land still looked desolate. Old men and women whose sons and daughters were killed had nowhere to go and as a result had remained by the ruins of their former villages, living in poorly repaired houses and planting small gardens which were frequently overrun and trampled by the cattle of the newly arrived Whites. Few adult males were in the almost deserted villages, although one was occasionally glimpsed going into or coming out of forests, obviously on a hunting expedition. Small plots which seemed to be grave sites were near the houses, far removed from traditional burying grounds. These had been made by those too old, too sick, or too young to carry the dead any further.

Uriah contacted the remaining Wind Clan members of the Talladega Village. These, though few, met in council to ask him how the Muskogees were dealing with the Whites in the Pitch Tree area. Uriah told them what his father predicted. Upon hearing this, they were not surprised, but wanted to know how they could help him and if he could help them. They said they could direct him to land speculators who appeared more honest than they had expected and they could advise him as to which pieces of land had in the past proved most productive and easiest to cultivate. They would ask him, in return, to help them in revising a document which had been in draft form for several years, but not yet finalized, since all Muskogee Chiefs could not agree on all the terms. Since he had told them he had legal experience they would trust him to translate the document into acceptable English legal terms and to take it to Wind Clan members in the Pitch Tree settlement to merge their document with other versions from other villages. This Uriah agreed to do and he told his granddaughter he had kept the original draft which, he said, he found simpler, more enforceable, and more logical than similar American legal documents. It read in his draft:

Muskogee Crimes And Their Punishments

Murder shall be punishable with death. The person who commits the act shall be the only one punished and only upon good proof.

Self-defense shall not be considered murder.

Stealing shall be punished as follows: For the first offense, the thief shall be whipped. For the second offense his ears shall be cropped. For the third offense he shall be killed.

If any person gives false testimony because of which another suffers punishment he shall suffer the same punishment which he caused to be inflicted on the one against whom he testified.

If any person gets drunk and wants to fight, he shall be tied up until he gets sober.

Prisoners taken in war shall not be considered or traded as slaves. Chiefs of villages shall see that they work, eat and live as do the Muskogees.

Prisoners who refuse to do the same work as a free Muskogee shall be whipped.

If any man should set his Negro free, that Negro shall be considered a free man by all in the Nation.

Uriah said he thought then, and continued to think so the rest of his life, that the Muskogees were more humane and wiser than many of the White judges whom he later met. He did as they asked, but the document was not published in revised form until two years later.

The document was, of course, totally disregarded by the State of Georgia, Uriah told his granddaughter. The document had been drawn up to stop the land cessation made by General McIntosh, who had, in complicity with his cousin George Troup, later Governor of Georgia, signed treaties ceding land to the State of Georgia. To the 16 treaties already signed by Muskogees from the Revolutionary War period until 1814, General McIntosh and a few of the chiefs of Lower Creek villages added treaties in 1814, 1818, and 1821. Because of McIntosh's treaties with the State of Georgia, chiefs of the Creek Confederacy voted further treaties ceding lands a capital offense. McIntosh was so warned.

Uriah said he looked at land with Wind Clan members and finally chose a parcel near the river just outside the former village which was fast becoming a White settlement.

During his eight-month stay in Talladega he met his wife. She too was a Muskogee/Irish mix. Her father was a Protestant Irishman whose father had immigrated the preceding century. Her mother was a Creek of the Bear Clan. He said she bore no resemblance to the Charleston maidens or matrons he had courted. She had no skill in fancy needlework, could not dance old or new French dances, and, indeed, had never been instructed very far in English nor learned anything but basic reading and writing. She could read some verses from the Bible, from which she had been taught basic reading skills, and could write her name. Ironically, considering the following events, she was named Senoia, after the beautiful Creek wife of General McIntosh's father, the first of his wives. But, Uriah said, she had more grace and genuine beauty than any of the females he had courted in Charleston. She did not apologize for her ignorance, but said learning to read anything but the Bible would have been useless, since there were no other books to read and even writing her name would be of little use, since she had not been called on officially to do so in all of her 16 years and doubted that she would ever need to do so, since she would need to sign her name only when she married and after that her husband would sign for her. Uriah said her reasoning amused him and he told her that it mattered not at all to him either.

He returned to the Pitch Tree Settlement, conferred with his father and returned again to Talladega where he bought land from the most honest land speculator he could find and where he pursued negotiations with Senoia's mother and brothers. They did not readily give consent to his marriage with their daughter and sister. They too had heard that the relations between the Whites and the Muskogees in Lower Creek Territory were becoming more and more violent. Rapes of Indian women and murder without punishment by White officials were frequent. Unless they felt that Uriah would reside permanently in Upper Creek Territory where life for Whites was more peaceful, they felt they could not be sure their daughter and niece would be safe. Uriah could not promise anything until he had seen his family safely moved into Alabama territory.

Uriah made several trips thereafter between Talladega and the Pitch Tree Settlement. At first his mother could not be persuaded to leave. When, however, raids, murders and rapes by White settlers became more frequent she feared for her daughters and she listened reluctantly to the logic of Daniel Pearson and agreed to move.

Her brother, Hoponika Futsakia, Truth Teller, on the other hand, intended to keep his family in their ancestral home. At the end of two years Daniel Pearson and Uriah had transferred most of their household goods as well as the goods from the trading post to a new location in Talladega. The move had been very slow because neither Daniel nor Uriah felt they could both be away from the Pitch Tree Settlement at the same time. The unsettled life and conflict between the Muskogee and the Whites required, they thought, one of them as well as Truth Teller to stay at the Pitch Tree Settlement for the safety of the women in the family and the young male, the last of the children, until the move was completed.

By the end of 1824, however, Uriah was again at the Pitch Tree Settlement to complete the sale of the trading post when he heard that the State of Georgia was to have a distinguished visitor. The Marquis de Lafayette, the friend of George Washington, the godfather and foster father of Lafayette's son, would, according to the news that arrived in Georgia via Savannah in the early months of 1825, make a grand tour of the 18 states in the United States of America. General William McIntosh's White first cousin, Governor George Troup, had been instrumental in persuading the Georgia General Assembly to invite Lafayette to arrive in Georgia and then travel through the State on into Alabama. It was said that he would travel through newly ceded territory in Georgia and Alabama where there were still Creeks and Choctaws living in ancestral territory.

Thinking such an occasion was one not to be missed, Uriah hastened to finish the sale of the trading post and went south with Hoponika Futsakia, Truth Teller, at the end of 1824 to see the great French general.

Chapter VII

Beginning of the End
March–May 1825

Uriah said that, at the time, he was too close to the events to see clearly, but at the end of his life he realized that the years 1825 until the end of 1827 determined the rest of his life and took from him the option of remaining a Muskogee. He said he had learned from traders bringing newspapers with them to Daniel's trading post that the French General Lafayette was to travel with Governor George Troup and William McIntosh's son, Chilly McIntosh, through Georgia and into the recently ceded section of Alabama, beginning at Marion, Georgia, and going next to an army fort, Fort Benning, near Columbus, Georgia, for festivities welcoming him to the state.

Uriah said he had read about General George Washington and the French General Lafayette while at the Presbyterian school in South Carolina. However, he wondered why General Lafayette would now return to the Colonies where he had helped defeat the British. He must, he thought, be an old man now, too old to fight. He had heard from his Uncle John that the French general's own people had had a bloody revolution after the Americans and had killed their king and queen. Why, he wondered, would he leave his own country, which must still need him to give advice and to speak the wisdom of the old, to come to this country where the White man, newly released from his own bondage to the British, were oppressing the Red Men much worse than the British had oppressed the people of the Colonies. Maybe, he thought, it was just the senile fantasy of the very old. He learned that Lafayette had been invited by the United States Congress, but Governor Troup, anxious to establish Georgia's position as a major State, had insisted that he be allowed to conduct him through Georgia and the newly acquired Muskogee territories in Alabama.

The party was to make its first stop on the way to Alabama near the border at a trading post owned by a White fur trader, one with whom Uriah's father, Daniel, had often done business. Managing to arrive just ahead of the Lafayette/Troup/McIntosh party, March 25, 1825, Uriah arranged to stay at the trading post on the edge of Fort Benning.

Uriah said that date would always stick in his memory because there had been a spring storm and he and Hoponika Futsakia were taking the air on the porch of the trading post. Lafayette's carriage, surrounded by the Georgia Militia, pulled up in front of the trading post and Lafayette descended, accompanied by his son and his secretary. While Lafayette and his son were escorted with great pomp and circumstance into the trading post, the secretary remained on the porch and started a conversation.

Uriah said the secretary introduced himself as Auguste Levasseur and asked their names. Uriah, was still wearing his Muskogee traveling clothes and, although he had intended to try to meet General Lafayette as a White man, he presented himself as Sakoeka, a Wind Clan Muskogee, and introduced his uncle with his Muskogee name also.

Uriah said that he was more than a little amused to read much, much later, when the events of those days had passed into history, both real and imagined, that the secretary had recorded the meeting. Uriah said that the secretary had written that there were two male Muskogees sitting at the door of the trading post, both "remarkable for their beauty and form" and that the younger of the two, Uriah, had been sent into the White man's world to be educated and that he spoke impeccable English. Uriah said he was sorry his father in Talladega was not alive when that tale was recorded and published at a time much removed from the events. He thought his father would have been both pleased and surprised that the secretary had praised his English. Uriah added that the last two comments of the secretary were pure fiction on the part of the secretary. Levasseur had written that Uriah had told him that he had returned to Indian land because he preferred their way of life and that he had married several Muskogee women in the Fort Benning area. Uriah also said that when Levasseur and his party, desirous of learning something immediate about Muskogee ways, asked them to perform some native dances, he and Truth Teller, both amused, invented some dances on the spot which they thought would impress the visitors as being savage. He added that he had never seen the dances they invented performed by any other Muskogees at any other time or place. Adding to their amusement was the offer of the Frenchmen to show them in return some French country dances. All in all, Uriah said, he and Truth Teller were pleased and amused by the encounter. The rest of the visit and trip of Lafayette and his group they found less pleasing and a great deal less amusing.

A later, very talented writer, he said, had written, almost 50 years after these events that the Indians in March 1825 during Lafayette's visit were "a little soured on a treaty that was made or was about being made with the Georgians."

Uriah said that the history of this treaty needed to be sketched so that Eva and the rest of his grand children as well as his nieces and nephews, would understand his part in the events of 1825.

"After the Muskogees lost the Battle of Horseshoe Bend in 1814 and were forced by General Andrew Jackson to cede 140,000 acres of land in Upper Creek Territory, there was reserved only a small strip of territory for Muskogees. Additional land had been ceded in 1819 and 1821 by the Lower Creeks under William McIntosh, Micco of Coweta Village. McIntosh and his White first cousin, George Troup, began planning the annexation of additional Indian lands once Troup had become Governor of Georgia in 1823.

"The Miccos of all towns in the Nation had met in council and had voted, again, that no further land cessation could be made without the complete agreement of all the chiefs of all Muskogee towns. When I was in Georgia and Alabama in March of 1825 this was the treaty which McIntosh had made February 12, 1825, against the united wills of most of the other Miccos. This was the reason that those who opposed him were 'soured' on this the Second Treaty of Indian Springs. Only ten percent of the Miccos had signed this treaty, named for McIntosh's major plantation. The First Treaty of Indian Springs had also been signed there. The Treaty was signed at a tavern and inn belonging to McIntosh, near a ferry, which McIntosh also owned. The treaty gave away all the remaining land of the Muskogees, both that of the Cherokees in northeastern Georgia, as well as those headed by McIntosh as Micco of Coweta Village. These were the same Cherokees who had helped the Americans in the War of 1812 against the British. This treaty and land cessation would begin the displacement of almost all Muskogees to land across the Mississippi River. McIntosh's plantations, The Reserve, and two other of his plantations were exempt from the terms of the Treaty."

Uriah said he did not know at the time what negotiations had transpired between McIntosh and his cousin George Troup.

As it happened he was later to act as a lawyer for both those opposing the treaty, called by the United States "The Hostiles," and even later helping other lawyers representing the McIntosh party against the Federal Government. In this capacity he was to be given access to documents detailing the events in Washington and in Milledgville. The intermediary between the President and the Governor of Georgia, George Troup, Duncan G. Campbell, wrote Troup from Columbia, South Carolina, January 31, 1825, stating that his return to Georgia had been delayed because the President had required him to consult with the Secretary of War. He reported:

"The application which I submitted for authority to hold a treaty with a divided council of the Creeks, was not expressly granted. Such a course, by a decision of the cabinet, was held to be incompatible with the laws of nations and Indian usage; every other facility, however, was promptly afforded. The sub-agent has been removed, the agent himself placed completely under our control, and our instructions so extended and liberalized as to authorize the most sanguine expectations of success. The negotiations will be renewed at the Indian Springs, on the 7th February. Orders to this effect were issued and forwarded from Washington City."

Prior to the anticipated negotiations and the "sanguine expectations of success" set down by Campbell, in his letter of January 31, McIntosh, representing his party from the towns of Coweta, Talladega, Cusseta, Broken Arrow, and Hitcheta, wrote to the President of the United States three weeks later from the Creek Nation, January 25, 1825, asking for protection against those Creeks led by Big Warrior who refused to participate in negotiations signing away further Indian land.

McIntosh, as Special Native Council, his son Chilly McIntosh as Clerk, and his son-in law, Sam'l Hawkins as Interpreter, told the President:

"We are informed that Big Warrior and his chiefs are now in council, and we expect are passing such decrees as are derogatory to the safety of McIntosh and the rest of his chiefs; for instance, it has been but a short time since they met in the grand council square, and passed an order for the execution of McIntosh, and any other of his chiefs who would make any proposition to the United States in favor of selling any part of the country we now claim; therefore we have been compelled to guard General McIntosh, since the Treaty at Broken Arrow, for his safety."

McIntosh goes on to demand that Big Warrior and Gun Boy, who also opposed the sale of land, be excluded from whatever negotiations were to be conducted between the United States and the Creeks, citing his party's loyalty during the War of 1812. In addition, he asked that the Federal Indian Agent, John Crowell, be removed, since he was too favorable to Big Warrior and those refusing sale of further land, maintaining the illegality of the Second Treaty of Indian Springs. Of the 35 Creeks signing the letter, only Joseph Marshall, Benjamin Marshall and John Shuman signed their names. All the others signed with an X.

About a week later, February 9, 1825, Governor Troup sent to D. G. Campbell and J. Merriwether, the United States Commissioners for holding treaty with the Creeks at Indian Springs, a letter from the President by express mail informing them of the President's recommendation to Congress.

They replied in part:

> *We cannot admit the possibility of defeat, yet such may be the result. Our expectations are founded upon facts which amount to the strongest assurance of success and we must indulge the gratification; that, even while 'Troup is Governor,' the policy and obligations of the United States will be effected, and the rights of Georgia obtained.*

Troup replied to the Commissioners that:

"There can be no doubt of the correctness… that a treaty concluded with that portion of the tribe resident in Georgia, for the cessation of all the lands within our limits, would be approved by Congress."

In their next communication with Troup on February 13, the Commissioners assured him that "*'the long agony is over,' and that we concluded a treaty yesterday with what we consider the nation, for nearly the whole country.*"

And as Troup had assured them, the treaty passed the Senate by one vote and the President signed it into law. Troup wrote to the Senators and Representatives in Congress from the Executive Department, Georgia, Milledgeville, February 17, 1826, a long letter, ending with:

"I understand that those of the tribe who refused their assent to the treaty threaten injury to Macintosh and his chiefs. Should the execution of these threats be attempted, (the treaty having been ratified,) I will feel it to be my duty to punish, in the most summary manner, and with the utmost severity, every such attempt, as an act of hostility committed within the actual territory and acknowledged jurisdiction of Georgia; and this whether the agent of the United States may think proper to deport himself as a neutral or a partisan."

Governor Troup followed this with:

A PROCLAMATION

Georgia:

By his excellency G. M. Troup, Governor and Commander-in-chief of the army and navy of this State, and of the militia thereof:

Whereas, by a treaty concluded with the Creeks, at the Indian Springs on the 12 of February last, their claims to the whole territory within the limits of Georgia were ceded to the United States; and the ratification of the same by the President and Senate having been made known to me; by which act the territory aforesaid, according to the stipulations of the treaty, and of the articles of agreement of cession of the year 1802, will, on or before the 1st day of September, 1826, pass into the actual possession of the State of Georgia.

McIntosh did not hear directly from Troup but read the ratification of the Proclamation in the newspapers. He wrote Troup, telling him so, and also told him that he had seen in the newspapers that John Crowell, the Federal Indian Agent, had told the President that only minor chiefs had signed the treaty and that if the treaty was ratified there would be retaliation against McIntosh's party. McIntosh also told Troup:

"We are not in any way in any danger until he (John Crowell, Federal Indian Agent) comes home and commences hostilities and urges it on himself."

He asked Troup to lend Samuel Hawkins, his son-in-law, 2,000 dollars toward the money due from the treaty in order to send Hawkins across the Mississippi to study the proposed site for the migration.

Ironically, Uriah said, the very Muskogees who had helped the Whites win the war with Britain were now not to be allowed to profit by the peace and prosperity gained by that war. Another irony, Uriah said, was that as he and his uncle were amusing themselves at Fort Benning at the expense of the secretary of the old French general, General McIntosh was, the next day, March 26, preparing to round up and sell his cattle and possessions. His agreement with his cousin, George Troup and the Georgia assembly were to award him not only the money promised to all Lower Creek Muskogees, but an addition sum for himself and the exemption of his main plantation and two others from the terms of the treaty. His major plantation, called the McIntosh Reserve, had also been exempted from sale with the First Treaty of Indian Spring in 1821. Although he had been warned and Governor Troup was aware of his precarious position as well of what would happen if further Muskogee land was sold, he could not have known the full extent of its repercussions. He wrote a letter on the 26th of March. Much later, when he was a lawyer helping the Muskogees in their attempt to petition the Federal government for redress of grievances, Uriah came into possession of the letter. The letter showed that McIntosh was very aware of his reputation among many of the Muskogees and Whites and was working against time. The letter, addressed to General Ware, of the United States Army, read:

> *26 March 1825*
> *"Gena Ware*
> *My friend I have instructed my son John & Benj Derriso to get me fore or five hed of horses & to promis cattle of any description for them being that I am in the Nation the people that is my settlement might be afraid to trust me I wish you to stand my security as you know me before I am in distress at this time to collect my cattle with So soon as I collect them I will give choice to any man that will be good enough to trust me of cows & calves steers or baron cows & so I wish you to stand my security to any bargains that they make. Nothing more I remain*
> *Your friend William McIntosh*

Uriah said that the fact that both Troup and McIntosh were aware of the death sentence pronounced against McIntosh by the majority of the Creek chiefs refusing to sign the Second Treaty of Indian Springs, made him a little less sympathetic toward him and his family once he had, of necessity, but reluctantly, become involved in McIntosh's fate.

But while McIntosh was preparing to liquidate his possessions, and gain additional funds by means of the projected treaty with his cousin and the State of Georgia, Uriah said he and Truth Teller joined the several hundred dignitaries and hangers-on who followed the party of Lafayette, Governor Troup and Chilly McIntosh, son of General McIntosh, from Georgia into Alabama.

When Lafayette's entourage came to the bank of the Cattahooshee, young men, Lower Creek Muskogees, stripped naked and, taking the place of the horses of Lafayette's carriage, swam the river, using ropes to pull the carriage with two lines of Indian braves. This scene, which much interested and amused the Whites, Uriah, and Truth Teller as Muskogees, found ignominious. To use Muskogee braves as beasts of burden for the White man did more than "sour" them against the dignitaries assembled. Their anger continued well into the events in the Lower Creek territory of the Pitch Tree Settlement and Indian Springs which transpired some five months later.

When the naked braves reached the top of the river bank, Chilly McIntosh introduced General Lafayette to the American dignitaries gathered to meet him. Afterwards, the entire assemblage marched to Fort Mitchell where the Muskogee Little Prince also greeted him. He told the young Muskogees gathered that they should entertain the French General with a game of stick ball, a fast, dangerous and reckless game requiring much agility and skill which was played naked. Not satisfied with the entertainment of the game, admired by all, the Whites treated General Lafayette to a visit with a notorious drunken Indian who amused the group by his broken English and his begging of a bottle of whiskey from the General, which he was given. This scene, which amused and delighted the Whites, angered and disgusted Uriah and Hoponika Futsakia and they left the party before it went on its way to Montgomery and Cahaba.

Still full of resentment, they returned to Pitch Tree Settlement, some 30 miles from where McIntosh was preparing to quit Georgia with his money and possessions and all the Upper Creeks who would go with him to the land promised them across the Mississippi River. After signing the Treaty of Indian Springs February 12, McIntosh by the end of February had still not finished settling his personal affairs, selling his horses and cattle, as well as accumulating his possessions from his several plantations. Had he left by the end of February or the beginning of March, he would have avoided his fate.

When Uriah and Truth Teller returned to the Pitch Tree settlement, they found chiefs from most of the Lower Creek towns and some of the few remaining from Upper Creek towns, assembled in council. The Second Treaty of Indian Springs had been agreed to by eight chiefs and others, not chiefs, assembled at McIntosh's Indian Springs plantation, a small minority of all the more than 50 Muskogee chiefs, who by common agreement were to accept or reject all treaties unanimously.

Several of those signing were relatives of General McIntosh, and most were not chiefs. Uriah, now a fully participating member of the council, tried at first to advise using caution, as he thought his father would have done. He told them that the treaty was not valid, since it was made with the State of Georgia, not with the Federal government of the United States, which had agreed that no further Muskogee lands would be settled by Whites. He, as a man who knew the White man's law, and others he knew who would volunteer to help, would write to the government in Washington, or go there if necessary and remind the White men and the Great White Father of their promises. This way, the Federal government could control the State of Georgia and compel Governor Troup and his cousin McIntosh to give up their plans for further expansion of White settlements without Muskogees, now too weak to protest, getting involved.

Most of the powerful chiefs were opposed to this advice. They reminded the members of the council of all the Muskogees had done to avoid trouble with the White settlers, of what the White settlers, admittedly not all, just the worst, had done to the Muskogee. They recounted the number of rapes of their daughters and wives, of the encroachment on hunting grounds of the Creeks and of murders of Creeks without any punishment of the murderers. They also reminded the council of the warning given in February to McIntosh and the other chiefs who comprised only about a fifth of all the chiefs who had signed this Second Treaty of Indian Springs. McIntosh had known what the penalty would be should they sign away any more of Muskogee territory.

Chiefs came and went from villages during the remainder of the month. Although there were few remaining great chiefs, all male members had a vote in the decision which would be binding on all members of all the Muskogee settlements.

Big Warrior, head chief of the Upper Creeks, was patient but reminded the Creeks that they must move before General McIntosh left Muskogee territory. Most were waiting in February to see if the Treaty would be signed by McIntosh and the Georgians.

Beginning in February, the chiefs tried to obtain a copy of the treaty and a list of the chiefs who had signed it. The list included few major chiefs, only eight, although more than 50 full Muskogee and half-breeds ultimately signed the treaty on the bar of the tavern owned by McIntosh.

Some chiefs questioned if those who signed had been primed with liquor, pointing out that some of those who signed were not chiefs, but relatives of chiefs among the assembled council chiefs. When, the chiefs assembled to study the list of signers saw the names of members of their clan, relatives by membership in the clan, there was sorrow and anger, but no attempt to change the judgment of the council. Uriah kept the following list the rest of his life, after he had taken the names to his mother, Sapehunka. All except McIntosh had signed with their X, since none of the signers except William McIntosh could read and write. These Muskogees signed:

SECOND TREATY OF INDIAN SPRINGS

Etommee Tustunnugee of Coweta;
Holahtau, or Col. Blue;
Cowtau Tustunnugee;
Artus Mico, or Roly McIntosh;
Chilli McIntosh;
Joseph Marshall;
Athlan Hajo; Tuskenahah;
Benjamin Marshall;
Coccus Hajo;
Forshatepu Mico;
Oethlamata;
Tallasee Hajo;
Tuskegee Tustunnuggee;
Toshajee Tustunnuggee;
Emau Chuccolocana;
Abeco Tustunnuggee;
HijoHajo;
Thia The Hajo;
Tomico Holueto;
Yah Te Ko Hajo;
No cosee Emautla;
Col. Wm. Miller,
Thleeatchca;
Abeco Tustunnuggee,;
Hoethlepoga Tustunnuggee;
Hepocokee Emautla;
Samuel Miller;
Tomoc Mico;

Charles Miller;
Tallasee Hoja, or John Carr;
Otulga Emautla;
Ahalaco Yoholo of Susetau;
Walucco Hajo, of New Yauco;
Cohausee Ematia of New Yauco;
Nineomau Tochee of New Yauco;
Konope Emautia, Sand Town;
Chawacala Mico, Sand Town;
Foctaluslee Emaulla, Sand Town;
Josiah Gray from Hitchatee;
William Kannard, from Hitchatee;
Neha Thlucto Hatkee, from Hitchatee;
Halathla Fixico, from Big Shoal;
Alex. Lasley, from Talledega;
Espokoke Hajo, from Talledega;
Emauthia Hajo, from Talledega;
Nincomatachee, fom Talledega;
Chuhah Hajo, from Talledega;
Efie Ematia, from Talledega;
Atausee Hopole, from Talledega;
James Fife, from Talledega.

Uriah pointed out to the council members that the treaty was illegal in more than one aspect. First, the treaty was signed by only a few of the chiefs, not the full membership of all Muskogee chiefs as was required by Muskogee law, and second, most of those at the end of the list were not chiefs and therefore had no right to speak and sign as if they were Muskogees still in possession of their territory in Georgia. Eight of those lived in Talladega, in Upper Creek Territory, already ceded.

Nevertheless, the council reaffirmed the unanimous vote to impose immediately the penalty which McIntosh had been told that he would subject himself to should additional Georgia lands be sold to the White man. The penalty was death and the judgment was carried out the day following the decision of the assembled chiefs in council, April 30, 1825. This was a little more than a month after the Second Treaty of Indian Springs had been ratified.

Those from the Pitch Tree Settlement to carry out the assassination, 50 Muskogees, were chosen by lot. Sakoeka/ Uriah and Hoponika Futsakia were among those chosen. Uriah said that even if he had not been chosen, he would still have been obligated to go, because this was the revenge which was required for his young uncle's death 11 years before at the Battle of Horseshoe Bend. He said he went with a heavy heart because this was not to be hand-to-hand fighting between men. The penalty required that everything belonging to McIntosh was to be destroyed or taken away. This included women, children, slaves and all livestock. Killing a man who is trying to kill you, he said, was one thing; killing the weak and helpless was another. Nevertheless, family duty and obligation impelled him to Indian Springs, some 30 miles from the Pitch Tree settlement.

Prior to starting the trip to McIntosh Reserve, the council had decreed that each village represented should contribute from 10 to 20 braves, more if they wished, and the assembled braves finally numbered between 100 and 200. Four Red Stick chiefs lead by Menauway, took charge of the party, each taking about one-fourth of the braves. Careful instructions were given that the respective parties were to arrive each from a different point of the compass and were to attack at the same time on a given signal. All males at the McIntosh plantation were to be killed even if they were not permanent members of McIntosh's household. Women and children were to be spared and taken away, if possible, but killed if need be. Everything belonging to McIntosh was to be destroyed and burned, all outbuildings, the main plantation house, all equipment of every sort. Cattle and horses were to be driven away to be collected later by the raiders. Slaves, of which McIntosh was said to have anywhere between 40 and 70 in all, were to be collected from the main plantation at McIntosh Reserve as well as from McIntosh's adjacent plantations, Lockchau Talofau, or Acorn Bluff, and put in charge of a party of Muskogees to be returned to the closest Muskogee settlement. There they would be distributed by lot. This they did in the early morning of April 30, 1825.

Uriah said that he and Truth Teller rode together with the band which was to attack from the west side of the plantation where there were outbuildings, barns, stockades, and buildings for storing farm equipment.

Just as they arrived, just before daybreak, somewhat before the others were in sight, Hoponika Futsakia spotted a man coming out of a latrine outhouse pulling on his trousers. He recognized the Tennessean who years before had attempted to sodomize Uriah. He motioned silently to Uriah and they both recognized the same burly, ill-kempt man who had joined their party in their trip across Georgia into South Carolina when Uriah first went to Charleston. He had been stopped from the attempted rape by Truth Teller, who had taken a small piece of flesh from his upper arm and warned him if he should ever come into Muskogee territory he would be killed for his attempted sodomy. Because the party had not yet been given the signal to attack, both Uriah and Hoponika Futsakia, at the same time, drew their bows and shot him with their arrows, not daring to use a gun which might rouse the plantation. Uriah said the man dropped without a sound, but the signal to attack, a loud war whoop by all the assembled Muskogees, sounded almost at that time and they had no time to examine the body.

To set fire to the plantation house and outbuildings, a Muskogee brave shot an arrow carrying a piece of burning material into hay stacked against a small barn. The fire lit up the entire area. This began the general massacre.

"I can't tell the exact events of the massacre first hand because my attention was directed toward herding those not of McIntosh's plantation or tavern away from the burning property. A recent thunderstorm had swollen the Chattahoochee River and some travelers in the region had taken refuge in McIntosh's tavern and inn located on the Federal Road and were waiting for the waters to recede. Hopenika Futsakia and I were herding them out in front of the plantation house to a clump of trees away from the burning buildings. Some of these were later to serve as witness to the massacre."

When he returned to the Muskogees burning and pillaging out houses, he saw that McIntosh, when he saw the raiding party coming, had come to the door at the front of the house with a pistol in each hand and two stuffed into his belt. He was accompanied by his friend, Thomas Tustunnuggee, who, standing in front of him, was immediately shot and dropped dead at the door. He saw two of his three wives, Peggy and Susannah, in the yard of the plantation house where they had been dragged, screaming. But when McIntosh saw more Muskogees coming from each side and at the back of the house, he retreated, shot and wounded, into the house and climbed up to the top floor. He began firing on the Muskogees below, but the hostile Indians had already begun shooting flaming arrows into the house. It caught fire almost immediately, setting the cedar shingles on the roof of the house ablaze. The smoke forced McIntosh to retreat back downstairs, where he kept shooting. All members of the attacking Indians within range fired on McIntosh as he ran out of the building to escape the smoke and fire. McIntosh kept firing as he ran, but within a few feet of the door dropped to the ground, hit numerous times. Uriah said he thought he had been hit at least 50 times, but other versions, including those of his wives, said about 100.

Uriah said whatever the number of shots McIntosh had received, he could vouch for the fact that McIntosh was defiant to the end and still alive when he fell. But, when he raised himself on one elbow to shoot one last time, the closest brave stabbed him in the heart. He died before he could get off the shot. In less than an hour, the wood plantation house and most of the outbuildings were burned to the ground and only the brick fireplaces were still standing.

General confusion and chaos spread throughout the yard and adjacent pastures and buildings as Indians pillaged and burned, gathered panic-stricken slaves, herded cattle and horses out of barns and corrals and took McIntosh's scalp, which was given to Menauway, the chief who had led the attack.

He said he went back with Truth Teller to examine the body of the Tennessean they had shot before the general attack. In the intervening years the Tennessean had gotten fatter and even more bedraggled and repulsive but Uriah thought he also looked pathetic. However, Truth Teller, who had no White blood and had been subjected to no Christian teaching which would have required him to understand and forgive an enemy, scalped the Tennessean and hung the scalp on his belt to be given to Sapehunka, now in Alabama. Uriah's mother had waited more than ten years for revenge and she was as steadfast in her hatred of her enemy as any Greek princess and she would have understood Electra and Ariadne.

He said he could not tell what happened in the next several days as well as McIntosh's wives could. When all was destroyed which could be destroyed, the hostile Indians left with whatever material possessions of McIntosh that could be carried and with their captured slaves. A small party was left behind to see that McIntosh was not buried and that even his dead body would receive whatever further insult the crows and vultures could inflict. One of his wives hovered over it to prevent the birds from further destruction. Another small party left to pursue the two who had escaped the house just as the party attacked, McIntosh's son, Chilly, and Moody Kinnard. A third party left to track down McIntosh's son-in-law, Sam Hawkins, husband of Jane, McIntosh's daughter by a Cherokee woman. They found Hawkins, kept him tied up, but later the same day killed and scalped him.

At McIntosh's Reserve during the massacre were two of his three wives, his Creek and Cherokee wives, Peggy, a Cherokee, and Susannah, a Creek. The events of the massacre as two of his wives recorded them, or dictated them to someone, Uriah said, were as he remembered them. He showed his granddaughter the letter some one had written of their behalf three days after the massacre. He said he had the copy of the letter as well as further correspondence from McIntosh's party from a White man, a representative of the Indian Agent, with whom he had collaborated in representing the Muskogees in their attempts the next few years still to keep, against all probability, at least a remnant of their land. It said:

May 3, 1825 Line Creek, Fayette County
To: Col. D.G. Campbell Maj'r Jas Meriweather
Gentlemen:

When you see this letter stained with the blood (the last drop of which is now spilt...for friendship he has shown for your people) I know you will remember your pledge to us in behalf of your Nation, that in the worst events you would assist & protect us, And when I tell you at day light on Saturday morning last hundreds of the hostiles surrounded our house and instantly murdered Gen's MIntosh and Thomas Tustunnuggee by shooting near one hundred balls into them (Chilly and Mooday Kinnard making their escape through a window) they then commenced burning and plundering in the most unprincipalled way so that here I am driven from the ashes of my smoking dwelling, left with nothing but my poor naked hungry children who need some immediate ade from our White Friends, and we lean upon you, while you lean upon your government. About the same time of the morning that they continued the horrid act on Gen's another party caught Col Sam'l Hawkins and kept him tied until about 3 o'clock, when the Chief returned from our house and gave order for his execution in the same way, and refused to leave his wife any implements to cover his body with, so that it was left to the fowls of the air and the beasts of the forrest and Jenny and her child are in the same condition as we are. this party consisted of Oakfuskies, Talledgas and Muckfaws… tho there were others with them. The Chiefs that appeared to head the party were Intock chungo (of Mockfaw) and Minnow-away, but I know not where he was from, who said they were ordered to do it by Little Prince and Hopthle-Yoholo, and that they were encouraged and supported in it by the Agent) Federal Indian Agent John Crowell) and Chiefs that were left after Big Warriors death, in a council at Broken Arrow, where they decreed that they would murder all the chiefs, who had any hand in selling the land and burn and destroy and take away all that they had, and then send on to the President that he should not have the land. I have not heard of the murders of any others, but expect all are dead that could be catcht, but by reason of a great Freshett on the Cattahoochee, they could not get Col Miller or Hagy McIntosh, nor the Darisaus, and they and Chilly are gon to the Govornor, our country is in a most ruined state, so far as I have heard (though by reason of the high waters—word has not circulated fast) all have fled from their homes in our parts and taken refuge among their White Friends & I learn that they are now at Gen'l Wares (near his place) from 150 to 200 of them are afraid to go to their homes to get a grain of what little corn they have to eat, and if you and your people do not assist us, God help us, we must die, either by the sword or by famine… This moment gen's Ware has come in & will in a few minutes start with a few men and a few Friendly Indians to try to get a little something for us to eat—I hope so soon as you read this you will lay it before the Govornor and the President... that they may know our miserable condition and afford us relief as soon as possible. I followed them to their camp about 1½ miles to try to by of them something to cover the dead with but it was denied me, I tried also to get a horse to take my little children, and some provisions to last us to the White settlement, which was given up to me and then taken back, and had it not been for some White men, who assisted in burying the dead and getting us to the settlement, we should have been worse off than we were, if possible. Before I close I must remark that the whole party so far as I know them were hostile during the last ware.

Peggy and Susanna McIntosh

Uriah said that it was not known which, if either, of the wives put into writing the letter or if, as he considered more likely, they dictated it to someone, since he did not think either was literate. Uriah said the help McIntosh's wives asked for and hoped would come immediately did not come for some time and then obstacle after obstacle was thrown up to keep them from receiving what the Governor and McIntosh had told them they would receive. Even though Governor Troup and McIntosh both had known the Muskogees would try to carry out the sentence which they had imposed should any further land cessation occur, McIntosh had apparently thought he could be out of Georgia and in the promised land across the Mississippi River before his enemies were prepared or dared to carry out the sentence. When it became obvious that the Governor and the State of Georgia would deliver almost nothing, Peggy, McIntosh's Cherokee wife, complained to the Cherokee Advocate, saying:

I do not blame the Creeks, the Creeks treat me well. The Cherokees treat me well—it was by Government my husband lost his life—Government say to my husband, 'Go Arkansas, go Arkansas, and you will be better off.' My husband wished to please the Government—my house is burned, myself and my children run—my children naked—no bread—one blanket is all—like some stray dog. I suffer, with one blanket I cover my three children and myself—the Government say 'Go!' The Indians kill him, between two fires my husband dies. I wander—the Government does not feed me—no home, no bread, nothing! Till Gen Ware gives me a home, I suffer like some stray Indian dog.

Uriah said at the time of the massacre he had other problems and he did not come into possession of McIntosh's wives' letters until he, as a White lawyer, was later named by a White commission to work as translator and as advocate for the Muskogees left in Alabama and Georgia after the death of Chief McIntosh. He knew the Georgia government might be slow in giving comfort and aide to McIntosh's children and wives, since McIntosh was dead and had served his purpose.

However, they would not be slow in following the war party and exacting punishment for the death of McIntosh. Aware of the possible penalty for his participation in the massacre, Uriah hoped that he would have been taken for a Muskogee, since he had been dressed as a Muskogee and his face was hidden behind black war paint. Nevertheless, he thought it prudent to return only briefly to the Pitch Tree Settlement and to start as soon as possible for Talledega and his family there dressed and acting like a White man. This, he said, he did and he thought the ruse was entirely successful, since no one ever seemed to connect him to the event and once in Alabama he was lost among the newly arrived White settlers.

When he returned to Talladega, he was able to gain the approval of Senoia's family, who thought that, as he was part of the party which had assassinated McIntosh, he would remain as far as possible from Lower Creek territory. They were married by the White man's law in the newly created Bibb County and were about to settle down when he received a letter from the representative of the Indian Agent, John Crowell. An honest man, Crowell had been opposed to further cessation of Creek or Cherokee territory, since the Federal Government had guaranteed both the Creeks and Cherokees that current and past treaties would be honored. The letter asked him to return to Georgia as soon as possible to help force Governor Troup, with legal remedies, to honor treaties prior to the illegal Second Treaty of Indian Springs. Uriah said the Agent pointed out that he, Uriah, as one-half Creek, knowing the Creek culture and language and a member of the Wind Clan through his mother, and having, most valuable of all, received a White man's education and now a lawyer, could render a service to his Muskogee people that even he could not.

The question as to whether his part in McIntosh's assassination and the destruction of his plantations was known was answered. It was obvious no part of what had happened to McIntosh had been attributed to him. Now to be asked to represent the remnants of McIntosh's family against the Federal government seemed more than ironic. Yet, as a Muskogee, for Uriah the choice was clear. Clinging to the White man's law was the only remedy. His mother, Sapehunka and his newly acquired in-laws were at first opposed to his returning to Georgia.

Uriah/Sakoeka decided, however, to disregard their advice and risk their disapproval and now work as a White man within the White man's law. The irony, he said, was that he was to be on both sides of the Upper and Lower Creek dispute. Since, he, as a Creek/Muskogee of the Wind Clan had participated at the McIntosh massacre, he now, as a White lawyer, was to try to help what remained of the McIntosh party hold the U. S. Government to promises made. When his granddaughter remarked that this was seemingly playing both ends against the middle, he was amused but agreed that her criticism was probably just. Nevertheless, that was how it was.

When he and his new bride arrived in Milledgeville, Georgia, the capital for the past ten years, he was introduced to the Indian Agent and given copies of correspondence from the McIntosh party to various entities from whom they could reasonably expect help. The correspondence began only two weeks after the assassination of General McIntosh and was addressed to the President by way of James Barbour, Secretary of War. They pointed out to him that they had been promised protection by the Commissioners representing the U.S. Government when they signed the Second Treaty of Indian Springs. But, they also pointed out that, instead of protection, a hostile party of Creeks, not prevented by the promised Federal troops, had attacked and killed their father and Etomme Tustunuggee. They continuing saying:

> *"The Commissioners told us…you would send a garrison to Chatahouchie River to prevent any encroachment on our lands, before we move west of the Mississippi. This never was done and we did not ask for it, because it was not thought necessary. Now we need assistance and claim performance of your promises.*
>
> *"We ask to have revenge for our blood spilt by a hostile party of Indians, and that the murder of our father, General McIntosh and Etomme Tustanugge may be investigated and the ringleaders punished.*
>
> *"We now look for your protection as it was promised by the Commissioners, without it we cannot prepare to go West of the Mississippi—about one hundred troops will be necessary.*
>
> *"If our Father the President does not protect his red children we shall be oppressed and many of us will be killed, we hope he will not deny his protection as promised by the Commissioners. We have trusted his promises and think he will not deceive us."*

Uriah said that this letter was signed only by Chilly McIntosh, son of William McIntosh, Interlifkey McIntosh, Ben Dourozow and Jim Dourozow. All but Chilly McIntosh signed with his X.

Uriah said another letter the same day, May 17, 1825, was sent to Georgia officials complaining of the Indian Agent, Colonel John Crowell. This letter was signed by even fewer Creek representatives. Chilly McIntosh and Interiefkey McIntosh, after complaining that Crowell showed partiality, they continued to say:

> *Col'n Crowell was opposed to the treaty at the Indian Springs and tried to prevent the Creeks from selling their land to the United States. He told them they should not give any long answers to the Commissioners, but only say 'They had no land to sell.'*

After this, Crowell went to Washington to explain to the Federal Government that the treaty was not legal and not binding on the Creek Nation. He reminded the representatives of John Quincy Adams, the new President, that the treaty had been approved in the Senate by only one vote.

The letter said that after Colonel Crowell returned from Washington, a Council of all chiefs of the Creek Nation was called. It continued to say: "*Within eight days after this council a hostile party attacked the house of Gen'l McIntosh & killed him & Etomme Tustenugee.*" The letter implied that Crowell had encouraged the assassination of General McIntosh. Governor Troup did more than imply. He demanded that Crowell be replaced as the Indian Agent and representative of the Creek Nation.

Some of the McIntosh party, though not represented by Chilly McIntosh's group, saw a different solution to the problem. Despairing of receiving help from the Commissioners representing the United States government in moving to the region beyond the Mississippi, they tried as a last resort, at the end of May 1825, to petition as beggars to retain almost worthless territory, most of which, they thought, the land-hungry Whites would not want. Uriah said that it was he, ironically, who was part of the group representing this faction of the McIntosh party when they met at Milledgeville, Georgia.

The letter was written in a tone of supplication, and addressed, not to the Federal Government, but to the Legislature of the State of Georgia. Uriah said that it was composed under the direction of an honest and generous man, lately of the Congress of the United States, and although several lawyers had helped in its composition, it was directed by and was in the hand of John A. Cuthbert. It said:

> *General McIntosh was our head & we were the body, & the hands & feet—But our head is now cut off; and we cannot move to that distant country & put ourselves in the hands of our enemies. The Nations who live there would watch (for) an opportunity to destroy us, before we could have time to procure the aid of our great father. The people of our own nation have now become our deadly enemies. After killing McIntosh and several other distinguished Chiefs, they have driven us from our homes, plundered our property, & threatened our lives. The people of our nation have now become our deadly enemies. They first became our enemies because in the late war, we were the friends of the white man; because we fought by the side of the white man & hazarded our lives, & spilt our blood in the same cause. They now threaten, & rob; & kill us, because we have followed the advice of our great father & sold our land to the Georgians. We are not safe with them, even near our White friends in Georgia; and we cannot be so blind as to put ourselves in their power in a distant land. We have now no shelter left us, but in the bosom of our White neighbors. While we hold the treaty sacred, we*

earnestly request you not to leave us, & our wives, & our little ones to starve to death, or to fall by the hands of our enemies. We propose to you to allow us, out of the late purchase, a small spot where we can lie down in safety, & get a living by our own labor. We are but few in number, & expect to find our safety only in peaceful conduct among you. We are moderate in our desires, & do not wish for the best of your land. We will be satisfied with a tract of country, on the east of the Cattahoochee, extending from some point, a few miles above the High Shoals, to the Horse Path, about forty miles in length & extending about twenty miles east of that river. The larger part of this tract is poor & mountainous. In exchange for this settlement, we will give up our share of the purchase money under the late treaty held at Indian Springs. We wish to raises stock, cultivate the soil & learn the useful arts of the White man. We will live quietly under our laws, & will faithfully perform any civil or military duties which you may tell us. In exchange for protection, we will fight with you against all your enemies. From being a powerful nation, we shall be only a handful of men. From owning a large & rich country, we will settle down on a narrow strip of mountainous land, but hereafter we will be content, if we can find safety and subsistence. We pray to the Great Spirit, to put kind & generous spirit & feeling into the hearts of the people of Georgia; & to tell them not to let an unfortunate & afflicted people be entirely ruined by friendship for them. We trust that the head men of Georgia, after making a great state out of lands that formerly belonged to us, will leave to men who have long been their friends, a little corner in which they live.

Uriah said that this letter, to his knowledge, was suppressed by Governor Troup's agents and never reached the Legislature of Georgia, and that other documentation given him indicated that the hopes of the other part of the McIntosh party, those still seeking revenge, were also not realized. In the spring and summer they continued to pursue an attempt to obtain revenge through the United States government well into the fall of 1825. In mid-summer, in July, two months after General McIntosh's death, the Creeks were now divided into two groups. The first was McIntosh's Party, whose members were demanding the aid of both the Georgia legislature and the Federal Government to impose the terms of the recent treaty and to protect them. They were asking Governor Troup to fulfill his promise to punish "in a most summary way" those guilty of McIntosh's murder, as he had promised in February if attempts against McIntosh were made. They were, in addition, asking protection from the second group, all the other Creeks who were not only opposing the Second Treaty of Indian Springs but suffering from the loss of their land and continuing to search for and kill those responsible for it.

Chapter VIII

Milledgeville 1825–1830

Uriah said he had told his wife, Senoia/Nicy, that they would be in Milledgeville just a few months until he had done what he could to help any Creek group, but particularly those opposing the illegal sale of Creek territory. As far as he was concerned, the Cherokees, since they had supported General Jackson and General McIntosh against the Upper Creek Confederacy, could speak for themselves. But, he said, the months turned into a year and the year into another year, and that into another and another.

Senoia, her Creek name and Nicy her White name, he thought, adjusted as well as could be expected of one from a small Creek village, made even smaller after the Battle of Horseshoe Bend, which had killed upwards of 800 male Creek warriors.

Many Creeks had migrated west, going to Louisiana, Texas, Arkansas, and Oklahoma in small groups, usually with an extended family, having given up hope of aid either from the friendly Whites or hope of receiving any compensation for their land. Whites had moved in, most being peaceful farmers. However, communal land had been broken up into individual farms; the farms had been fenced; the forest and its creatures had been reduced by too many hunters who killed indiscriminately, destroying both those needed for food and anything in their gun's sight. The old ways of the Creeks were disappearing. The old, the sick, the crippled and the young were no longer taken care of by the clans. Disease, poverty, and sometimes near starvation could be occasionally seen, usually if the young male members who were to replace those who had been killed in the battles ten years before were not yet old enough to take care both of their parents, their grandparents, and their own young children.

Uriah said that the Georgia Legislature lost no time converting the Creek lands into counties and beginning a distribution of land by lottery. Although these were laid out, they were not named until December 14 of 1826, after the Treaty of Washington in 1826. Some of the land had been for several years illegally occupied by White settlers even before the Treaty of Indian Springs of 1825 was drawn up and signed. In just five weeks after the assassination of General McIntosh, on June 9, 1825, the State of Georgia added the five new counties later to be named Carroll, Coweta, Lee, Muskogee, and Troup.

Uriah's granddaughter remembered her grandmother as a beautiful, frail woman with a merry laugh, a sardonic smile and, sometimes, a malicious sense of humor. Her grandfather agreed with her analysis of his wife's character, but he added that these were the qualities that helped her to survive in Milledgeville in 1825 through 1830.

He said that although there had been an initial attempt to lay out Milledgeville after the logical and pleasant plan of Savannah, the cotton boom halted their plans and by 1825 the ten-year-old city had spread uncontrollably in all directions. The Capital, the first public building in the United States in the Gothic style, was grand and imposing, but its grandeur was surrounded by crowded inns, gambling houses, houses of prostitution. There were occasional duels on main street because of women or politics. Nicy was able to detach her Creek/Irish self from the chaos of life there and, sardonic and laughing, she would ironically remind her husband that they were only going to stay a few months. In fact, Uriah said, they stayed until after the birth of their second child and were not to leave until just before the birth of their third.

By October of 1825 the McIntosh Party still had not been able to secure any of the help promised from the Georgia Legislature. George Troup, a Jacksonian Democrat, was interested only in enforcing the illegal Second Treaty of Indian Springs.

Troup, formerly Governor of Georgia, had served as a Georgia legislator and as a member of the United States House of Representatives. He had been elected by a narrow margin, mainly by his promise to remove the remainder of the Muskogees to west of the Mississippi and to open up their land for White expansion.

Two delegations, one representing the Creek Nation of the McIntosh Party, as it was now called, and the other, headed by the Federal Agent for the Creek Nation, John Crowell, this group now called the Hostiles, left for Washington about November 22, 1825, at the request of President John Quincy Adams.

Since it was still necessary to secure a Federal passport to travel through Indian Territory, the McIntosh Party was somewhat behind the Indian Agent in being issued the following:

> *The Savannah Republic November 22, 1825*
>
> *General Gains has gone on I understand to Washington. Crowell who was also here a day or two since with a deputation of hostiles, has also proceeded for the same place. A portion of the deputation of friendly Chiefs will go tomorrow for the same destination. The—of their—-the death of McIntosh—their forlorn situation—their determination to obtain justice upon the murderers. Chilly McIntosh, Roley, Durasso, and Tustin-*

neggee, Speaker of the Nation, are among those here and bound to Washington. They are to be passed.

Uriah drafted, along with other older and more experienced lawyers, documents for the Creeks not of the McIntosh party, now called the Hostiles, to present to the President and the Powers in Washington City proving that the Second Treaty of Indian Springs was not valid and violated previous treaties of the Creeks with the Federal Government.

He said as each of the events of the following two years unfolded, he thought more and more of the advice of his father, Daniel Pearson, to the Pitch Tree Creek Settlement council which Truth Teller delivered to them before he had left for South Carolina. He was reminded that his father had maintained that neutrality was the only way the Muskogees could survive, just as the great Tecumseh had said that an alliance of all the tribes in the continent was the only protection from the White man. He had also said that supporting the British or the Americans would not help the Muskogee to retain their land, because whichever side won, the Muskogee would lose. And that, Uriah said, was what happened even when a great and good President intervened.

Representatives of the Hostile Creek had managed to have their legal documents presented to John Quincy Adams, now President, who had the treaties with the Muskogees, particularly the First and Second Treaty of Indian Springs reviewed in Washington. He found them flawed and ordered that all surveying of Indian lands be immediately halted.

Meanwhile the McIntosh Party continued in Washington to push for approval and ratification of the Second Treaty of Indian Springs by the Federal Government, it having already been ratified by the Georgia Legislature by a wide margin and in the United States Senate by a single vote.

They arrived in Washington City early in January 1826, and

with their arrival and the arrival of the Indian Agent, John Crowell, before them, there began debates and disagreements as to who represented the Creek Nation.

The McIntosh Party found that the Federal Government was as little given to honoring its promises to them as was the Legislature of Georgia in promising them protection before and after the assassination of General McIntosh. The Secretary of War had decided that the Second Treaty of Indian Springs was invalid and presented a revised treaty to the McIntosh party to sign. They refused to sign, indicating the reasons why. They wrote from Washington on January 24th, 1826:

> *Washington Jan'y 24th, 1826*
>
> *The undersigned Friends & Followers of the late Gen'l William McIntosh having red to them a Treaty concluded this day between James Barbour Secretary of War & and the Delagation now in Washington, from the Creek Nation hereby subscribe their assent to such articles in said Treaty so far as they are interested. We refused this and the conference was broken up, they declaired that it was immaterial whether they (we) signed it or not—We declined signing it, first because we believe it made us to declair that our great Chief & our other Chiefs had acted without authority in signing the Treaty of Indian Springs—and second because the compensation for property and improvements was limited, to such as was in the ceded lands. No consideration will tempt us to degrade the memory of our great Chief nor to empeach the rightful acts of those who survived and our claim to compensation in our property is we think, not to be denied on principal of Justice—Our interpreter Hawkins at the close of the above conference took the paper they required us to sign to interpret to the Chiefs of the Delegation, which Gov. Cass said he might do, but told him not to show it to any body else—It was for this purpose and for this only that the paper was taken by Hawkins—for we could not think of*

signing such a paper, aney more than we could recouncile it to our feelings to take by the hands the murderers of our Chief as they proposed to us—

We will add a single remark—Col. McKenney addressed us simply as representatives of the friends & followers of the late General William McIntosh & speaks of our adversaries as 'The Delagation of the Creek Nation' Now we think it necessary to distinctly say to you, that we are not mearly the Friends and Followers of gen'l McIntosh, but that we are & have been for many years acknowledged chiefs of the Creek Nation and that we have not, nor have those whom we represent delegated any power to those whom he has distinguished as the Delegation of the Creek Nation.

Witness We remain your
Friends and Brothers,
John P. Denney
Chilly Mc Intosh
Rowley X McIntosh
Hathla Marta X Tustanuggee
Ben X Derrozow
Okin Occ a cha X Marthla
Ni-hi-o-hadu X Coweta
Arreb ca X Tustanuggee
Husput X Harjo
Aleck X Lassley
Benjamin Hawkins, Interpreter

Uriah said the delegates of the Creek, those not of the McIntosh Party, but those who were trying to protect and retain their land, culture, and life, told him when they had read the letter of the McIntosh Party of January 25 and the following one of January 26, they thought the McIntosh Party was beginning to realize that they would be reversed in Washington. Although they were still maintaining that McIntosh and the other Creeks had a legal right to sell the land of all the Muskogees, even though the treaty violated Muskogee law, they seemed to be trying to open negotiations for redefining the terms of any new treaty in order to retain the money they had received, be allotted more, and hold on to McIntosh Reserve and the other Reserves which were defined in the Second Treaty of Indian Springs.

Uriah said the letter of January 26, 1826, tried to make clear the position of the McIntosh Party and to protest the fact that the Washington authorities were supporting the Creeks, now called the Hostiles, who wanted the Treaty nullified and wanted to stay in control of what remained of Creek territory.

Washington D. C.
Jan'y 26, 1826
Friend & Brother:

We have received from Col. McKenny a letter dated January 25, 1826, in which he observes that he esteems it proper to correct an error into which he says we have fallen—He tells we were neither asked to sign the treaty which you have recently concluded with our adversaries, nor any notes that might be affixed to the same, but as that we had given an anamious but verbal consent to certain conditions on which we would emigrate to the Mississippi which had in all respects been complied with it was thought that it would look better, not for us to sign the treaty, or notes to be affixed to the same, but a seperaate paper sustaining that assent with our names—Sir, We are desireous if correcting the error of this statement & and for purpose we are making the following—

When we were first invited to talk to Gov. Cass (Governor of the Michegan Territory in charge of Indian Affairs) whether we were willing to emigrate & if so on what terms, we answered that we were willing to do so in terms of the Treaty of the Indian Springs—It was the request from us if that Treaty was annulled, on what terms we would be disposed to go, & we answered saying that we would take time to consider, but still insisted on the validity of the former Treaty—We then requested that the proposition of Gov. Cass should be given to us in writing, which was refused us—If this our request had been complied with, no dispute wud now occure, as to what had passed between us, we subsequently gave in our propositions and when we afterwards met Gov Gass & Col. McKenney at the office of Indian Affairs & have read what they proposed, we thought it correct—They then read to us a small of the paper which we afterwards found when they read the Treaty was a different instrument from what we understood it to be, we then found that provisions were inserted in a Treaty made with our enemies, by which you had declared that the Acts of our Great Chief & other Chiefs of the Treaty of Indian Springs to be null & void & by which you, as we understood, had departed from the terms which they had been recently read, by providing that the compensation for property & improvents in the ceded land. They then required us to sign an instrument in the following terms.

Uriah said that with sad hearts and no conviction, he and the other lawyers in Milledgeville began a draft of the last treaty, a revised treaty, now called the Treaty of Washington. They were aided by Superintendent of Indian Affairs in Washington, Thomas McKinney, and the Indian Agent, John Crowell. It was finished a year and a half later on November 15, 1827, and was known as the Treaty of the Creek Indian Agency. By it the Creeks gave up claim to all their territory in Georgia. Prior to the completion of the treaty, Troup was going ahead with the lottery, whereby all land, even if still inhabited by Muskogees, was divided into sections for White settlers. Many Creeks fought back, but they were outnumbered by the waves of Whites, and so rapes, pillaging, and murders came with the White man.

The Upper Creek delegation agreeing to the new treaty was headed by Chief Opothleoholo. Uriah said it was more favorable to the Creeks in remuneration for losses, but it preempted all Creek territory except a small portion. As originally drafted, the Upper Creeks were to retain all their territory until January 2, 1827, and then move to a smaller section between Alabama and Georgia. All Creek territory on the east side of the Cattahoochee River, Lower Creek territory belonging to General McIntosh's Party, would be ceded. The entire Creek Nation was to receive $217,600 dollars and a promised payment annually of $20,000. In addition, the treaty provided financial remuneration for the losses caused to the Lower Creeks in the fight of McIntosh's Party against the rest of the Creek Nation. The McIntosh Party would not only share in the money paid and promised to the Creeks, but would also be given funds for a five-party delegation to go inspect the territory west of the Mississippi allotted them and, upon their approval of the territory, they were promised that the United States Government would fund the relocation, giving a full year's subsistence for all the Lower Creeks, provide a full-time Federal Indian Agent, interpreter, blacksmith and wheelwright.

The Treaty signed on January 24, 1826, and ratified by the United States Senate on April 22, 1826, disappointed many of the Upper Creeks, but Uriah said he and the others who had been instrumental in trying to retain Creek land felt that the agreement was the best, under the circumstances, that could be had. He said he did not then know the reaction of McIntosh's cousin, Governor George Troup, nor the final terms of the Treaty signed on November 15, 1827, concluded between James Barbour, Secretary of War, and Chief Opothleoholo of the Creek nation. It was finally signed by Thomas L. McKenney and John Crowell on behalf of the Creek Indian Agency and by Little Prince with his mark on behalf of the Creek Nation.

Had they known, they might have held out for better terms and retention of territory in spite of and against the arguments of the Federal Government and the State of Georgia.

He did not know until much later that when White settlers from Tennessee, Kentucky and other states to the north moved into and encroached on Creek hunting grounds and villages, Troup set up agencies, in principal to hear and pass on to the President of the United States any grievances of the Muskogees. In fact, while some did just that, they also followed the grievances with a disclaimer, stating that they only witnessed signatures of the chiefs and did not believe or subscribe to their complaints. The WESTERN CREEK AGENCY, on March the 23rd of 1829 sent the following up the line of command to Colonel D. Brearley:

> *Sir:*
>
> *At the request of the officers of Cantonment Gibson, I beg (have sic.) leave to state they wish it to be distinctly understood by the President of the United States that they were only witnesses to the acknowledgement of the signatures of the Creek Indians who signed the Memorial respecting their grievances; as & also to disavow any participations, approval or belief that their charges and speculations are correct; they disapproval of the charges but could not refuse to sign as witnesses to the signatures…Whereas Mr. Lott, old Sam'l Berryhill and many others refused to sign—old John Berryhill opposed the Memorial in Council but was forced to sign by the Chiefs.*

Having put himself on the right political side, the writer goes on to add matters he considers more important. He adds:

> *The Steamboat Facility, Capt Pennanette arrived here three days since and is now aground at the Mouth of the Grand River where she will probably remain for sometime. She has*

about 15 tons of freight (furs) on board belonging to Col Chouteau who is going down on—to New Orleans

Lt. Dawson was married to Miss Baylor on Tuesday night last and she is still alive.

We have just finished the issue or rations to the 6th of April—and I have the pleasure to say that we are all in good health.

God bless you and may you prosper in all your arrangements.

Sincerely, your friend
Thom. Anthony

Chapter IX

States Rights vs. Federal Law

1830–1839

Uriah said that after the Treaty of Washington, the Creeks were known as Western Creeks (Upper) and Eastern Creeks (Lower). And even while legal wrangling and shifting positions were occurring in Washington, and while many of the McIntosh Party had begun a slow migration to the lands across the Mississippi, Chilly McIntosh and Roger Tiger began acting as agents for Western Creeks, buying and selling land allocated to them by Lewis Cass, the United States Land Commissioner in the last treaty.

In 1833, for example, he witnessed the Deputy Clerk for the Superior Court of Muskoggee County enter into court records two such transactions. The first was for five sections of land transferred to Chilly McIntosh's cousin, Benjamin Hawkins, and John Milton for $2,000 dollars and 25 sections of land transferred to the same buyers for $20,000. Both were dated the 1st day of June 1833. The first guaranteed, "the said Chilly McIntosh and Robert Tiger, acting as agents aforesaid of the said western Creek Indians, according to the power of attorney hereunto annexed, the said bargained premises unto the said Benjamin Hawkins and John Milton, will warrant and for ever defend the right and title thereof against themselves and against the claims of all other persons whatever." However, the second said: "if the deed already on this day made shall not be adjudged valid, or if after the location they desire another deed, and will surrender that already given, or to their assigns."

Uriah said that the United States Supreme Court in 1832 in the case WORCESTER V. GEORGIAN rendered a decision overturning a lower Georgia court decision against a settler, Samuel A. Worcester, and others in Gwinett County in the State of Georgia in which the defendants were found guilty and sentenced to four years in Georgia prisons. Worcester was found guilty for "residing within the limits of the Cherokee nation without a license" and "without having taken the oath to support and defend the constitution and laws of the state of Georgia. The Supreme Court answered the question: "Does the state of Georgia have the authority to regulate the intercourse between the citizens of its state and members of the Cherokee nation?

The Court answered, "No," giving as its reasons the following as delivered by Chief Justice John Marshall:

> *The Georgia Act, under which Worcester was prosecuted, violated the Constitution, treaties and laws of the United States. Treaties and laws of the United States contemplate the Indian territory as completely separated from that of the states, and provide that all intercourse with them shall be carried on exclusively by the government of the union."* Justice Marshall argued: *"The Cherokee nation, then, is a distinct community occupying its own territory in which the laws of Georgia can have no force. The whole intercourse between the United States and this nation, is, by our constitution and laws, vested in the government of the United States."*

The Georgia act thus interfered with the federal government's authority and was unconstitutional. There was only one dissenting vote, that by Justice Henry Baldwin.

Governor Troup, Uriah said, paid not the slightest attention to the Treaty of Washington and, backed fully by the Georgia Legislature, had surveyors begin immediately to survey all Muskogee land, including the small portion between Georgia and Alabama reserved for the remainder of the Creeks, in preparation for lotteries to be held to distribute or sell all Indian lands in Alabama and Georgia.

Adams, given his authority as the President of the United States authorized by the Constitution to make treaties and have them ratified by the Senate, sent a lieutenant in the United States army, Lt. J. R. Minton, to hand deliver a letter to Governor Troup commanding him to halt all surveys immediately and ordered the United States Attorney for the State of Georgia to have anyone attempting the surveys arrested.

In addition, President Adams threatened to send Federal troops into Georgia to enforce the Treaty of Washington. Uriah said he and the other lawyers in Milledgeville working on behalf of the Hostile Creeks thought such power would sway even the self-willed cousin of General McIntosh, Governor Troup. The President trying to uphold the Treaty of Washington, wrote, with copies to the Hostile's attorneys:

> *The pretensions under which these surveys are attempted are in direct violation of a treaty, and if persevered in, must lead to a disturbance of the public tranquility.... The President will feel himself compelled to employ, if necessary, all the means under his control to maintain the faith of the nation by carrying the treaty into effect.*

Uriah said the Creeks should have known that Troup would not abide by any Federal command which was contrary to whatever he and the Georgia Legislature had decided.

And, that was what happened. Troup called President Adams' hand, saying that if the President sent Federal troops to the sovereign State of Georgia:

> *"From the first decisive act of hostility, you will be considered and treated as a public enemy. You, to whom we might have constitutionally appealed for our defense against invasion, are yourselves the invaders, and, what is more, the unblushing allies of the savages whose cause you have adopted."*

He then ordered two divisions of Georgia militia on alert to defend the State of Georgia against a possible Federal invasion, saying,

> *"The argument is exhausted; let us stand by our arms."*

And, like many another good, but weak, man, President Adams, wanting to see justice done, but thinking that he himself could not help do it, gave in to powerful men in the United States Congress, friends of Governor George Troup, and commanded the Indian Agent, John Crowell, to begin writing yet another treaty.

Uriah said that he and the other lawyers in Milledgeville conferred with Crowell, who told them that from what he had seen and heard in Washington, it appeared that Jackson and his Democratic Party would win the next Presidential election and, therefore, he had no hope that any treaty with the Muskogee would hold, no matter what its terms. Both President Adams and members of Congress, whatever their private opinions, deemed that justice to the Muskogee was not worth risking a civil war and possible loss of the good opinion of the White voters.

With sad hearts and no conviction, Uriah said the other lawyers in Milledgeville began the last treaty, aided by the Superintendant of Indian Affairs in Washington, Thomas McKinney, and the Indian Agent, John Crowell.

It was finished a year and a half later on November 15, 1827, and was known as the Treaty of the Creek Indian Agency. By it the Muskogees gave up all claims to their territory in Georgia. Prior to the completion of the treaty, Troup was going ahead with the lottery whereby all land, even if still inhabited by Muskogees, was divided up into sections for White settlers.

Many Creeks fought back, but they were outnumbered by the wave of Whites, and so rapes, pillaging, and murders continued and increased with the increase in White settlers.

Uriah said that Truth Teller's wife had died early in 1826 and although he tried to persuade him to come to Talladega, where Daniel and he could possibly protect him, he refused, and with his two sons, now adult Muskogees but not married, he went to join the Seminoles still fighting the United States forces in Florida, and all three perished there.

McKinney had offended General Jackson by continuing to assert that the Muskogees were, in intelligence and morality, equal to the Whites, contrary to Jackson's opinion that they were savages, little better than animals. The one decent thing the treaty did, Uriah said, and this he thought was the work of Crowell and McKinney, was to set up provisions for the continuation of schools for Muskogee children at the "Chocktaw Academy" in Kentucky and two other schools, the Withington and the Asbury, all under the Department of War. The treaty was signed in two parts. The first part had the following signatures:

Thomas L. McKinney
John Crowell
Little Prince, his X mark
Epau-emathia, his X mark
Tinpouchoe Burnard, his X mark
Hathlan Hojo, his X mark
Oke-juoke Yau-holo, his X mark
Cassetaw Micco, his X mark

These were signed in the presence of Luther Blake, secretary, Andrew Hamill, Whitman C. Hill and Thomas Crowell.

The second part of the treaty provided for the schools and for carts, wheels, blankets and other articles necessary for the Creeks to begin their trek at the onset of the winter out of Georgia into lands across the Mississippi. The treaty was signed in various Indian towns which Uriah listed for his granddaughter.

John Crowell

BROKEN ARROW TOWN: Little Prince, his X mark, Tuskugu, his X mark, Cotche hayre, his X mark

CUSETAU TOWN: Tukchenaw, his X mark, Epi Emarthis, his X mark, Oakpushu Yoholo, his mark; COWETAU TOWN: Neah Thieuco, his mark

TOMASA TOWN: Colitchu Ementia, his X mark, Arthlau Hayre, his X mark, Cowetaw Micco, his X mark

OSWICHU TOWN: Halatta Tustinuggu, his X mark, Octiatchu Emartla, his X mark, Charles Emarthia, his X mark

UCHEE TOWN: Timpoeche Barned, his X mark

CHAWACCOLA HATCHU TOWN: Coe E. Hayo, his X mark, Powas Yoholo, his X mark

Ema Hayre, his X mark

The witness of the second part of the treaty were Luther Blake, secretary, Andrew Hamill, Enoch Johnson, Thomas Crowell, Benjamin Marshall. The interpreters were Paddy Carr and Joseph Marshall.

Uriah said that after this treaty was signed there was little to do on behalf of his people except to help Thomas Crowell see that the terms of the treaty giving money and other compensation to the Creeks were carried out. The Cherokees, long assimilated into the White frontier culture, were beginning to be harassed, but it was not until two years later that General Jackson, now President Jackson, made his demands even harsher, but at first only strongly suggesting that the Cherokees and the remnants of the other Five Civilized tribes move across the Mississippi. Uriah said that wherever he and Senoia/Nicy lived, he always kept two speeches framed on his office wall or in his dining room, so as to always to be reminded of and to remind his sons of the moral superiority of his uncle, Hoponika Futsakia/Truth Teller, to White men in general and to President Andrew Jackson in particular.

Shortly after becoming President in 1829 Jackson delivered this speech to the Creeks:

> *Friends and Brothers—by permission of the great spirit above, and the voice of the people, I have been made President of the United States, and now speak to you as your Father and friend, and request you to listen. Your warriors have known me long. You know I love my white and red children, and always speak with a straight, and not with a forked tongue; that I have always told you the truth. I now speak to you as my children, in the language of truth. Listen.*
>
> *Where you now are, you and my white children are too near to each other to live in harmony and peace. Your game is destroyed and many of your people will not work and till the earth.*
>
> *Beyond the great River Mississippi where a part of your nation has gone, your Father has provided a country large enough for all of you, and he advises you to remove to it.*
>
> *There your white brothers will not trouble you; they will have no claim to the land, and you can live upon it you and all your children, as long as the grass grows or the water runs, in peace and plenty. It will be yours forever. For the improvements in the country where you now live, and for all the stock which*

you cannot take with you, your Father will pay you a fair price.

Where you now live, your white brothers have always claimed the land. The land beyond the Mississippi belongs to the President and to no one else; and he will give it to you forever.

Uriah said no Muskogee would ever have given the name Hoponika Futsakia to Andrew Jackson. Neither did Chief Speckled Snake, who answered Jackson's duplicity and hypocrisy. He said the second speech which he put on his walls wherever he lived was Chief Speckled Snake's ironic speech to the Creeks.

Chief Speckled Snake told the Creeks:

Brothers! When the white man first came to these shores, the Muskogees gave him land, and kindled him a fire to make him comfortable. And when the pale faces of the south (the Spanish) made war on him, their young men drew the tomahawk and protected his head from the scalping knife.

But when the white man had warmed himself before the Indian's fire, and filled himself with the Indian's hominy, he became very large. He stopped not for the mountain tops, and his feet covered the plains and the valleys. His hands grasped the eastern and western sea.

Then he became our great father. He loved his red children; but said 'You must move a little farther, lest I should by accident tread on you. With one foot he pushed the red man over the Oconee, and with the other he trampled down the graves of his fathers.

But our great father still loved his red children, and he soon made them another talk. He said much; but it all meant nothing, but 'move a little farther; you are too near me.'

I have heard a great many talks from our great father, and they all began and ended the same.

Brothers! When he made us a talk on a former occasion, he

said, 'Get a little farther. Go beyond the Oconee and Ocmulgee. There is a pleasant country. He also said, 'It will be yours forever.'

Now he says, 'The land you live on is not yours. Go beyond the Mississippi. There is game. There you may remain while the grass grows or the water runs.

Brothers! Will not our great father come there also? He loves his red children, and his tongue is not forked.

Chapter X

Blue Remembered Hills

Into my heart an air that kills
From yon far country blows:
What are those blue remembered hills,
What spires, what farms are those?
That is the land of lost content,
I see it shining plain,
The happy highways where I went
And cannot come again.
—A. E. Housman

Uriah said that at the beginning of 1835 Nicy/Senoia and he with their sons had moved back to Alabama, to Talladega where his mother, Sapehunka, now about forty-three, and Daniel Pearson, now fifty, had reestablished themselves with a prosperous trading post on the McDowell Ferry Road in Fayetteville. Their two daughters had married White men from families originally from North Carolina. The last child, a son, had now been sent to Charleston, South Carolina, to live with John Pearson and his wife, Lucinda, where he attended a new Presbyterian school, less classically oriented than Uriah's former school, but much praised by Charleston's aristocracy, of which both John Pearson and Lucinda, she reluctantly, were members. Lucinda's father, George McGowan, had grown old happily with his aristocratic wife on his 5,000 acre plantation, later expanded to 10,000 acres.

Established as a lawyer in Talladega City, Uriah said he read in newspapers President Jackson's Second Inaugural Address of May 28, 1830. He said he wondered in amazement how Jackson could declare to a civilized nation that he had always had the red man's interests at heart.

In his address, Jackson wandered through rehearsals of diplomatic arrangements with Great Britain, Spain, Russia, and Mexico, provisions and plans for canals and ended with the announcement of the Indian Removal Act to the Congress.

Uraih said he copied out some of the pronouncements which were the most outrageous. He said that, if nothing else, he would bequeath these to his descendants. These were:

> *It gives me great pleasure to announce to Congress that the benevolent policy of the Government, steadily pursued for nearly 30 years, in relation to the removal of the Indians beyond the white settlements is approaching to a happy consummation... It will separate the Indians from immediate contact with settlements of whites, free them from the power of the States, enable them to pursue happiness in their own way and under their own rude institutions, will retard the progress of decay, which is lessening their numbers, and perhaps cause them gradually, under the protection of the Government and through the influence of good counsels to cast off their savage habits and become an interesting, civilized and Christian community.*
>
> *Toward the aborigines of the country no one can indulge a more friendly feeling than myself, or would go further in attempting to reclaim them from their wandering habits and make them a happy, prosperous people. ...What good man would prefer a country covered with forests and ranged by a*

few thousand savages to our extensive Republic, studded with cities, towns, and prosperous farms embellished with all the improvements which art can devise or industry execute, occupied by more than 12,000,000 happy people, and filled with all the blessings of liberty, civilization, and religion?...

And is it supposed that the wandering savage has a stronger attachment to his home than the settled, civilized Christian? Is it more afflicting to him to leave the graves of his fathers than it is to our brothers and children? Rightly considered, the policy of the General Government toward the red man is not only liberal, but generous.

And, Uriah said, with just one more paragraph, Jackson condemned the Muskogee to perpetual exile and hastened to inform the Congress of revenues to extinguish the public debt. His hypocritical hopes for the well being of the Muskogees ended with:

May we not hope, therefore, that all good citizens, and none more zealously than those who think the Indians oppressed by subjection to the laws of the states, will unite in attempting to open the eyes of those children of the forest to their true condition, and by a speedy removal to relieve them from all the evils, real or imaginary, present or prospective, with which they may be supposed to be threatened.

There had been some, mainly Christian missionaries, who fought against the Act; some such as missionary Jeremiah Evarts, led several movements agitating against the passage of the Act. It was also opposed by United States Senator Theodore Frelinghuysen and Congressman David Crockett of Tennessee (who had been present with Jackson at the Battle of Horseshoe Bend and had written "We shot them like dogs.").

Jackson, for the rest of his term as President, created, with the Democratic Party, the Spoils System, and forcing his economic policies through the Federal Congress caused the Panic of 1837, which was followed by a seven-year-long recession, the worst until that time. "Old Slickerly," true to his character, admitted no wrong-doing.

The first removal after the signing and affirmation of the Removal Act was the Treaty of Dancing Rabbit Creek, September 27, 1830, signed by the Choctaws of Mississippi. The second was that of the Treaty of New Echota, signed in 1835, which sent the Cherokees on the trail to Oklahoma. More than 600 had left during the winter of 1834 prior to the signing of the treaty and of these almost 200 died from the cold, exposure, and inadequate clothing. Before the next group reached Oklahoma more than 4,000 men, women and children had died, including the leader, Chilly McIntosh, son of General McIntosh.

Chief Yoholo Micco (also known as Chief Eufaula) spoke to the Alabama legislature in 1836 just prior to the last removal of the Creeks from ancestral lands,

> *In these lands...which have belonged to my forefathers and where their bones lie buried, I see that the Indian fires are going out. Soon they will be cold. New fires are lighting in the West for us, they say, and we will go there. I do not believe that our Great Father means to harm his red children, but that he wishes us well.*

He died on the way west. As general, President and a human being, Jackson, it would much later be said, "makes the blood run cold."

Here, Uriah broke off his story saying to his granddaughter that he would tell a little of the story of Hoponika Futsakia and the Seminoles' war against the Whites at another time. Now, his mind was turning back to Daniel Pearson, to Truth Teller, to the Great Tecumseh and what might have been in the blue hills and mountains of the Muskogee.

Chapter XI

Epilogue

When Uriah's mind turned back to his early life, the time before the last war through which he had lived and in which he and his sons had participated, the War of Secession, called the Civil War by the government in Washington, he said that the removal of the major portion of the Creeks to Oklahoma, Mississippi, and Texas did not end the conflict between the Whites and the Muskogees.

The Seminoles of Florida, cousins of the Creeks, had supported the British in the War of 1812. They had for years been trading for weapons with the British prior to that time when Florida was a possession of Spain. He said he had heard, but rarely had the information confirmed, that the Seminoles, the name in Creek meaning wild, runaway, outlaw, or crazy men, had their name from a long ago fight between the Creeks and the Yemasses. The Creeks won the battle, but some of the young men took wives among the Yemasses and began the Seminole tribe. These were later joined by outlaws from many nations and by run-away slaves fleeing the United States.

By the time of the Indian Wars, these were a formidable nation and the last to hold out against the incursion of the Whites and the army of General Jackson. While the Creeks in

Alabama and Georgia were losing battles and land to the U. S. army and the influx of settlers from the states north of Georgia and the Carolinas increased until by 1817 they arrived in greater and greater numbers each month, the Seminoles were preparing for war.

After crushing and removing the Muskogees from Alabama, Georgia, and the Carolinas, Andrew Jackson invaded Spanish Florida fighting against the Muskogee Seminoles and Black African Seminoles there. With an army of 3,000 Jackson destroyed Seminoles villages, leaving behind the dead and dying Seminoles to move forward to attack Spanish settlements and capture the Spanish forts at St. Marks and at Pensacola. His success there caused the Spanish to negotiate a treaty with the United States in 1819. John Quincy Adams as Secretary of State and Spain's minister Luis de Onis signed a treaty ceding Florida to the United States and nullifying the 5,000,000 dollar debt Spain owed the United States.

The victorious General Jackson was charged with setting up a United States government in Florida. He divided Florida into East and West Florida. Leaving Florida, he turned the government over to William Pope Duval.

Northern settlers immediately began invading Florida, clashing with the Seminoles in Tallahassee. The government asked the Seminoles to move. They refused. Florida had become a United States territory in 1822. In 1823 a treaty, the Treaty of Moultrie Creek, between the Seminoles and the government required the Seminoles to move south and to agree to discontinue hiding run-away slaves. The Seminoles were given 4,000,000 acres of land south of Ocala. Their former home, Tallahassee, became the new capital of the territory.

When Jackson became President of the United States in 1829, some Seminole chiefs were tricked into agreeing to look at land west of the Mississippi, but when they returned they claimed they had been tricked and refused to move. Their leader, Osceola, led a surprise attack against the Americans when a Major Dade was leading forces from Fort Brooke and Fort King. More than 100 soldiers were killed.

It was at this point that Truth Teller, his wife and his two sons, as well as Mabry, the Black/Creek and his family left the Muskogee settlements in Georgia to join the Seminoles in their fight against General Jackson's forces in Florida. There were more than 30 Seminole settlements in Florida, most pure-blooded Muskogee, but at least three totally Black Seminoles. In all, the total number of Seminoles not surrendering was estimated at about 300.

Just as Daniel Pearson before him, Uriah tried to persuade Truth Teller to join him in Talladega, where the Whites and Muskogees seemed to be achieving peaceful settlements. But, as John Pearson would have understood, Truth Teller preferred freedom with dignity as a Muskogee to bending to the will of the Whites, particularly Andrew Jackson and George Troup.

The move to Florida was unusually dangerous for Mabry. Black Seminoles villages were raided and captured Negroes were sold into slavery, some having ancestors who had never been enslaved by the American Whites. One of the most active in pursuing the Black Seminoles was Roly McIntosh, one of the richest slave holders among the Creeks.

Osceola, defeated and captured in 1837, died in an army prison in Charleston in 1838. Here Uriah halted to add:

"I was ashamed of my half-white ancestry when I heard Osceola was captured when he came under a flag of truce to parley with the Whites."

Another Seminole leader was luckier than Osceola. That any Seminoles survived, particularly Black Seminoles, was due to Osceola and to the fact that about 500 Black Seminoles had accepted the promise of freedom if they would migrate to the Indian Territory in Oklahoma.

The second rebel leader of the Seminoles after Osceola was

Coacoochee, Wild Cat. Coacoochee had been captured with Osceola when they had come to parley with the American commander under a flag of truce, but, luckier than Osceola, he escaped. He continued to harass the military, but finally, seven years after his first capture with Osceola, he was finally defeated and sent to Arkansas.

He said at his departure, "I am alone. I am going to my new home in Arkansas. I have thrown away my rifle and buried my hatchet. With the bright eyes of my sister looking at me at the pebbled bottom of my own Ahapopha, I have washed the dark stains of blood from my clothes and person, and I now say unto my white fathers, take care of me."

And so they did, until December 1845, when the military needed him to go on a peace mission to the Comanches in Texas. For the next four years he traveled through Texas and Mexico. He tried to get other Seminoles in Florida to join him in Mexico.

Roly McIntosh, who profited by the traffic in captured Seminole Blacks sold into slavery, complained to the Military, "Now he (Coacoochee) come back with enticing news and want to carry his people to that nation; and the negroes, he told them if they emigrate to that country, they will be freed by the government. This is good news to the negroes. I am told some are preparing to go. Wild Cat held council with his people—had this talk with them."

In 1849, he joined some southern Kikapoos and migrated permanently to Coahuila, Mexico, where he died of smallpox in 1857.

The Seminoles had lost their battle with General Jackson and the United States forces, but some did not admit defeat and fled further into the Everglades and continued a guerrilla fight until 1858.

Although the first and second Seminole wars were lost and many were forced to migrate to the lands west of the

Mississippi, some few, usually estimated at about 200 to 300, retreated into the Everglades, and never surrendered. Truth Teller and his sons died among that number. Before his death and that of his two sons, he sent his two grandchildren, sons of one of his sons, back to Talladega to his nephew Uriah. He asked him only that they be reared as Muskogees and not as Whites. Given the changing times, Uriah complied with his request so far as was possible.

Uriah said that for him and his family the period from the end of 1836, when the last Creeks were forcibly removed from their ancestral homes by Andrew Jackson and the U.S. Army, was relatively peaceful and prosperous. He and the other lawyers having failed to convince Washington of the illegality of Jackson's removal of the Cherokees and Creeks, he settled into the life of a gentleman farmer and lawyer in Talladega.

Settlers continued to flow in yearly from the states north of Georgia, Alabama, and Florida. Some brought enough money to buy small plots of land; others participated in the land lottery established by the government and received free or almost free land. Plantation owners extended their holdings, bought more slaves and rented out unused land to settlers having no money and no ability to buy land of their own. These settlers gave 50-percent of their crops to the owner of the land. Having no contract and no established tenure, they migrated from year to year from one land owner to another, rarely managing anything but bare subsistence.

Lucinda's father, George McGowan and his aristocratic wife had died, leaving Lucinda owner of his holdings, which had increased many times the original 5,000 acres he had initially built his plantation house on.

His uncle John Pearson had sold his mercantile business, keeping their Charleston town house as an escape from the humid Charleston summers and moved to the plantation to oversee Lucinda's inheritance. John was satisfied with their new existence, but Lucinda found herself with more slaves than she could personally care for and educate and was never completely happy with the new life. As slave births continued, the numbers grew and there were too many to house and feed. Some had to be leased out to other land holders, further distancing her from her slaves. John and Lucinda's sons grew up on the plantation, became managers and owners as they matured and John retired to his, by now, extensive library. Their daughters married sons of other plantation owners, and they became part of Charleston society and forgot their origins. Only Uriah and his family were left to remind them that they had mixed breed relatives.

Private life for all the Pearson/White and Pearson White/Muskogees was peaceful and prosperous from 1836 until April 12, 1861. The Recession precipitated by Andrew Jackson's economic policies, lasted from its onset in 1837 until at least 1848. Hard times added to the contention between the industrial North and the agricultural South. But even before the outbreak of open warfare, there was very little peace between the States either at the State or Federal level.

Slavery, compounded with economic issues between the agricultural South and the manufacturing North, divided the States and the population. Now it was no longer Massachusetts threatening secession from the union of States, saying it was better to amputate a gangrene limb than to lose the whole body but many, and finally all of the Southern States.

Both Uriah's parents had died surrounded by Uriah's Pearson and Senoia's Muskogee families.

As tensions increased between the States, the fires were fanned by those on both sides exploiting the situation. Uriah felt more and more like his father. Just as his father in 1811, he in 1860–1861, then more than 60-years-old, foresaw the coming conflict. And, just as his father had feared he would join the Red Stick warriors in their fight to retain their land and way of life, he feared his three sons, all now married, would join those from the South now ready and anxious for war with the Yankees.

Just as the Creeks had fought desperately to save their land and way of life, the Southerners, many of whom had taken the Indian lands, fought to save the land that had now become their own. And, just as the Creek lands were occupied by Federal troops, so were the Southern States after they lost the war. Federal troops came to "reconstruct" the South, despising the Southerners' way of life just as Jackson had despised that of the Muskogees.

Eva said she knew her grandfather only when he was a very old man, but one of her cousins, older than she, said that one incident on the plantation during Reconstruction had stuck in his memory. When in Charleston in his law office, Uriah dressed as a cultivated White man, but on the plantation he dressed as a Muskogee. Once, having returned earlier than expected from Charleston, and having already changed into his Muskogee clothes, he saw a young Federal officer blocking the front door of the plantation house where a young niece was trying to enter. Early Muskogee training had endured. He threw his hunting knife and accurately pinned the young officer's jacket sleeve to the door facing. Angry and blustering, pulling the knife out of the door facing and releasing his sleeve, the officer threatened Uriah, "Old man, you'll die soon, and a grown man will be needed to take care of and defend these young girls. You'd better treat the Federal troops better if you don't want worse things from them than a little friendly conversation with your women."

Contrary to the young Yankee officer's prediction, Eva said, Uriah lived to see the end of Reconstruction and his descendants re-established in the new South. Before he died, however, at nearly 88, he reminded Eva that the people of the Southern States had exercised what they considered their right given by the DECLARATION OF INDEPENDENCE. Thomas Jefferson had written:

> *"When any form of government becomes destructive of these rights (life, liberty, and the pursuit of happiness), it is the right of the people to alter or abolish it, and to institute new government, laying its foundation on such principles, and organizing its powers in such form as to them shall seem most likely to affect their safety and happiness."*

The Federal government paid no more attention to that statement than Andrew Jackson had to the decision of the Supreme Court as delivered by Chief Justice John Marshall and Troup had paid to John Quincy Adams' decision that Georgia had no control over the Muskogees, who were a sovereign nation.

And once again during the "Reconstruction" of the South, there were, as there would be many times in the future, servants on horses, folly set in great dignity, and princes walking as servants on the earth.

THE END

About the Author

Nina Cooper holds a Ph. D. in Contemporary Literature from the University of Texas at Austin. She has done work on the theatre of Gabriel Marcel and Jean-Paul Sartre as well as on the short stories of Julien Green.

Her translation of Emile Gaboriau's *Monsieur Lecoq*, published by Black Coat Press, appeared June 1, 2009. Translations of Gaboriau's *File No. 113* and Fortuné du Boisgobey's *The Omnibus Crime* will be published by Distinction Press in 2010.

www.ingramcontent.com/pod-product-compliance
Ingram Content Group UK Ltd.
Pitfield, Milton Keynes, MK11 3LW, UK
UKHW020133250726
13967UKWH00002B/624

9 780980 217544